S

Γ

NOTES

including
- *Life of the Author*
- *List of Characters*
- *Introduction*
- *Evolution of the Text*
- *Critical Commentaries*
- *Character Analyses*
- *Themes and Symbols*
- *Questions and Essay Topics*
- *Selected Bibliography*

by
Carol H. Poston, Ph.D.

INCORPORATED

LINCOLN, NEBRASKA   68501

Editor

Gary Carey, M.A.
University of Colorado

Consulting Editor

James L. Roberts, Ph.D.
Department of English
University of Nebraska

ISBN 0-8220-1241-3
© Copyright 1974
by
C. K. Hillegass
All Rights Reserved
Printed in U.S.A.

1993 Printing

Cliffs Notes, Inc.   Lincoln, Nebraska

CONTENTS

Life of the Author 5

List of Characters 10

Introduction 14

Evolution of the Text 16

Critical Commentaries

    Book 1 18
    Book 2 30
    Book 3 51

Character Analysis 62

Themes and Symbols 68

Questions and Essay Topics 73

Selected Bibliography 75

Life of the Author

Francis Scott Key Fitzgerald's origins are a peculiarly American distillation. From his father came the historic names, Scott and Key, and a family who had been in America since the 1600s. His mother, Mary McQuillan, was of Irish immigrant descent, but her family had made much money in the new land. And, although Princeton prestige and New York parties come to mind at the mention of his name, Fitzgerald was actually a midwesterner, born September 24, 1896, in St. Paul, Minnesota. His father was not prosperous, and the family moved to Buffalo, New York, when Scott was two, to Syracuse, New York, when he was five, back to Buffalo when he was seven and a half, and finally, in 1908, when he was twelve, back to St. Paul, where the family remained.

Young Fitzgerald early knew the terror of a lack of money. Before the final move back to St. Paul, his father had been fired by the firm of Procter & Gamble. The elder Fitzgerald's failure no doubt haunted the young man, but, at the same time, in his father he sensed quiet good taste and natural courtesy and decorum, values which he transferred to Dick Diver's father in *Tender is the Night*. From his sire he also learned a great deal about the Civil War, a passion which supplies many references in that novel as well.

While still a student at St. Paul Academy, Fitzgerald began to write both stories and drama, though he did not seem to be interested in his regular courses. In an attempt to encourage him in more traditional scholarly endeavors, his aunt sent him in 1911 to Newman Academy, a Catholic boarding school in New Jersey.

Unpopular at Newman, partly because of his egoistic and braggart personality and partly because of his athletic ineptitude, he seems to have been labeled a "sissy," an important fact in view of his later harshness on homosexuality in his novels and because of the fear that he himself might be homosexual. He took relief from school in excursions to New York to go to the theater. Soon he was writing plays of his own, and the amateur productions of them, in addition to the editorship of the college paper and other honors, restored his popularity. He prepared to enter Princeton in the fall.

In September, 1914, he settled into the university, which had been his goal ever since he had heard of the Princeton drama club, the Triangle. He immediately became involved in writing a musical for the club. That work and his writing for the campus humor magazine, *The Tiger,* took up most of his time, but these activities took their toll, for he managed to fail several courses. Nonetheless, by his junior year his hopes were high: he expected to be the Triangle Club president his senior year, he had been placed on the editorial board of *The Tiger,* he had been admitted to a distinguished social club on campus, and he was in love with Ginevra King, a beautiful heiress from Chicago. But in November, 1916, he was forced to withdraw from Princeton because of his grades; he himself preferred to think that his removal was for health reasons.

By the time he returned to Princeton the following fall, his romance was breaking up and his ambitions were coming to naught. During his senior year, the war beckoned, and he left Princeton without a degree, but with rich imaginative materials for his future novels and with at least one lasting friendship, that of Edmund Wilson, the now famous author and critic.

The army did not send Fitzgerald to the front; he got only as far as Alabama, where two crucial things happened. He began working seriously on a novel which he had started at Princeton (later to be published as *This Side of Paradise)* and, most important, he met Zelda Sayre.

Zelda was the toast of Montgomery, a vivacious blonde who had hordes of suitors. Despite her solid and respectable family (her father was later a judge on the Supreme Court of Alabama),

Zelda Sayre was unconventional and daring, fond of reckless enterprises, such as appearing in a flesh-colored bathing suit, a joke which Fitzgerald later used in *Tender is the Night.* Fitzgerald fell in love with her and proposed immediately.

Wanting both to finish his novel and win his chosen woman, after his discharge in February, 1919, Fitzgerald returned to New York to become a writer. But fame was not easy to come by, and he was forced to write advertising copy to make a living. Finally, in order to complete his novel, he left New York for St. Paul, where he immersed himself in his work. The novel was accepted for publication by Scribner's in September, 1919.

In November, 1919, he became informally engaged to Zelda, who was still in Montgomery. Many biographers insist that Zelda demanded Scott's success as a writer as a prerequisite to marriage. That judgment seems unfair, since, though they were married in April 3, 1920, just after the first edition of *This Side of Paradise* had sold out, she had agreed to the marriage in November, 1919, when neither fame nor money had yet arrived for F. Scott Fitzgerald.

Success came almost too quickly. Though Edmund Wilson, for one, thought that *This Side of Paradise* was immature, Fitzgerald was catapulted to fame by the novel. The couple lived in luxury in New York and became the center of a sophisticated and exhausting social life where money — and alcohol — were in abundant supply. The publication of two volumes of short stories, *Flappers and Philosophers* (1921) and *Tales of the Jazz Age* (1922) and a novel, *The Beautiful and the Damned* first serialized, then published as a book (1922), added materially to Fitzgerald's income.

Though his books were selling well, the Fitzgeralds seemed to spend more money than they earned. They left for a visit to Europe in May, 1921, for a brief rest, and their daughter, "Scottie," was born in St. Paul in October, after their return. By fall of the next year they had decided to move back East; they settled in Great Neck, Long Island, where a close neighbor and friend was Ring Lardner, the famous short story writer, whose profligate brilliance was later used in the characterization of Abe North in *Tender is the Night.* Their social life remained riotous, and Scott was often drunk. Nonetheless, he kept working; he was hoping for financial success from a play, *The Vegetable,* which opened in November, 1923, in Atlantic City. It was a dismal failure, and Fitzgeraĺd was forced to write short stories, which were quick-selling and remunerative, in order to get out of debt.

While at Great Neck he worked on what was to become an American masterpiece, *The Great Gatsby,* and in the spring of 1924, when they were financially able to do so, the Fitzgeralds moved to Europe, where he hoped to finish his novel. In Paris they met Gerald and Sara Murphy, to whom *Tender is the Night* is dedicated, and after whose life style, in some measure, the Divers' was patterned. The Murphys took them to their hideaway on the Riviera, and there Fitzgerald labored to finish *The Great Gatsby,* which was finally published in April, 1925.

The novel's brilliance was recognized immediately by the critics, but it did not sell as well as Fitzgerald had hoped. It should be said that Fitzgerald made large amounts of money by writing, even during the lean years of the Depression; the fact remained, however, that the two usually spent more than they could earn. And in order to keep his income high enough to meet ever-mounting expenses, Fitzgerald wrote short stories and even went to Hollywood to write film scenarios.

Ironically, *The Great Gatsby* marked the end of Fitzgerald's fame as a writer. Dissipation had taken its toll, and he seemed unable to discipline himself for an extended artistic effort. In the meantime the Fitzgerald marriage, marked by recklessness and extravagance from the beginning, had yet a new strain — Zelda's dissatisfaction, which finally manifested itself as serious mental illness. Zelda was not without talent, but she was without an identity of her own in her marriage to a famous writer. To counter her feeling of uselessness, she tried a number of things, including painting, writing, and practicing ballet avidly. While she continued painting for the rest of her life, it was a limited pursuit because of her failing vision. Her deepest commitment was to dancing, but she finally became aware that she had simply started too late for a serious career. Disappointed and exhausted from her ballet practice, she collapsed in the spring of 1930. Finally diagnosed as a schizophrenic, she was hospitalized off and on for the rest of her life until she died in 1948 in a hospital fire. After her institutionalization, however, she continued to write, and in 1930 she published her only novel, *Save Me the Waltz*, a highly autobiographical work which treats the trip to Europe and the stay on the Riviera, among other things.

F. Scott Fitzgerald's version of the story, a novel which had been in production for years, was at last published in 1934. *Tender is the Night* did not sell well, possibly because the American public, reeling under the weight of the Great Depression, was not in a mood for a tale of wealthy and privileged people. Fitzgerald was under severe financial pressure again, and he went to Hollywood once more to write his way to solvency. There he met Sheilah Graham; their love had become by the end of his life a quiet domesticity. She tried to give him some sense of order and attempted to aid him with his nearly hopeless alcoholism. He suffered a heart attack in late November, 1940, and the afternoon of December 21 he experienced the second and fatal one. He was buried in Rockville, Maryland, December 27, but because he did not die within the Catholic Church he was denied the last rites of the Church, which he had desired. His grave is not in the small cemetery with the generations of Scotts and Keys, but rather in the Rockville Union Cemetery nearby.

Before his death, Fitzgerald had been working on *The Last Tycoon*, a novel about his life in Hollywood; his old friend Edmund Wilson edited it and also a collection of personal writings, *The Crack-Up;* both volumes were published in 1945. Little attention was paid to this fine American artist until the publication in 1949 of Arthur Mizener's landmark biography, *The Far Side of Paradise*, triggered a Fitzgerald revival. The last two decades have seen F. Scott Fitzgerald placed in the pantheon of great American novelists.

List of Characters

Rosemary Hoyt

Beautiful American ingénue who has just succeeded in a Hollywood film.

Elsie Speers

Rosemary's calculating and opportunistic mother.

Luis Campion

A homosexual Englishman who is vacationing at Gausse's Hotel.

Royal Dumphry

Another homosexual who later appears suspiciously in the presence of Senor Real's son Francisco.

Albert McKisco

A writer and critic whose works are derivatory and watered-down versions of more famous authors.

Violet McKisco

His limited, yet ambitious, wife.

Mrs. Abrams

A cheerful, elderly American lady who is among the guests at Gausse's.

Dick Diver

The promising young psychiatrist whose fall from fortune forms the main interest of the novel.

Nicole Diver

The wealthy American woman whose mental illness first involves Dick Diver and, before she is completely cured, he marries her.

Lanier and Topsy

The Diver children, a boy and a girl.

Abe North

An American composer who, alcoholic and uninspired, has has not been able to write anything for seven years.

Mary North

His patient wife who later marries a moneyed Hindu to become the Contessa di Minghetti.

Tommy Barban

An acquaintance of the Divers whose business is war; he eventually seduces, then marries, Nicole.

Earl Brady

A movie actor whom Rosemary visits while he is making a film on the Mediterranean.

Collis Clay

A young Yale student, enamoured of Rosemary Hoyt, who first appears in Paris with the Divers' party.

Maria Wallis

An acquaintance of the Divers who shoots an Englishman in the Parisian railroad station, the Gare Saint Lazare.

Freeman

A Negro restaurateur arrested mistakenly for having robbed Abe North.

Jules Peterson

Another Negro who had seen Abe North robbed; he is killed for complicity in confessing to the whites.

Franz Gregorovius

A Swiss psychiatrist who becomes Dick Diver's partner in a new clinic.

Kaethe Gregorovius

His domestic and plodding, though jealous, wife.

Doctor Dohmler

The director of the Dohmler clinic; he originally interviewed Nicole's father and admitted Nicole for treatment.

Devereux Warren

Nicole's wealthy Chicago father; he is guilty of incest with his daughter.

Baby Warren

Nicole's wealthy, calculating and unmarried sister.

Nicotera

Rosemary Hoyt's leading man in a film being shot in Rome; the man who will probably be her fiancé.

Senor Real

A Spanish nobleman who brings his son to a Swiss clinic to be cured of homosexuality.

Francisco

Senor Real's young homosexual son.

Lady Caroline Sibley-Biers

The decadent English noblewoman whom Dick Diver rescues, with Mary Minghetti, from what seems to have been a lesbian escapade.

Introduction

Throughout the discussion of this novel, there has also been a consistent attempt to interlace relevant biographical information into the body of criticism about the novel. Such a practice could be discredited by followers of the New Critics school of literary criticism, who hold that the text itself is all important and should have no historical or biographical ballast to support it. Fitzgerald's novel, however, seems to become richer, more complete, and, at some points, more understandable if it is viewed against the backdrop of biography. We know, for example, from his notebooks that the author intended the Nicole Diver sections to parallel Zelda Fitzgerald's mental breakdown. This fact alone contributes a rather sizeable, and interesting, biographical element. Fitzgerald was one of those writers who created out of himself; something got written because he felt it deeply and personally. For this reason one often misses historical scope and philosophical depths in his writing, while at the same time one is grateful for the piquancy which his personal experience gives to his art.

This guide is also in some ways a feminist reading of *Tender is the Night* (a fact which might terrify the unwary student who intends to crib part of this for a term paper). What is a feminist critique and is such a thing justified in this instance? Actually, the fact is that what has passed for objective criticism in the past has nearly always had its bias—frequently masculine, so that "pure criticism" is rare. "Feminist" criticism does not mean the automatic dismissal of male characters from consideration. Instead it insists that criticism be balanced by an examination of females as well. F. Scott Fitzgerald called *Tender is the Night* "a woman's book," yet it has, nearly without exception, been examined solely in terms of its male hero. There has been an attempt here to look at the female characters as well, to examine Fitzgerald's portrait of them, and to sort out what seems to be a rather complicated authorial thesis about the nature of the male/female relationship.

Finally, a feminist reading in this case means giving some thought to Zelda Fitzgerald and trying to realize the influence she had upon her husband. A very useful purpose is served by reading her own novel, *Save Me the Waltz,* published four years before *Tender is the Night,* since the two novels treat many of the same events from the Fitzgeralds' life together. Even though her novel was rather heavily edited by her husband out of the fear that she was writing *his* novel, enough parallels remain to exhibit, rather dramatically, that F. Scott Fitzgerald often used his wife and her experiences rather mercilessly for his fiction. All these reasons make it clear that it is necessary to look critically at Fitzgerald's women. Indeed, such an examination broadens the scope of the novel and yields a better understanding of its author.

Evolution and History of the Text of "Tender Is the Night"

Tender is the Night's history constitutes a veritable saga of textual changes, changes which did not stop even with F. Scott Fitzgerald's death. And since there are two versions of the novel presently in print, it is a potentially confusing situation for the student. The fact which must be realized is that there is no definitive text for *Tender is the Night*.

Fitzgerald had the germ of an idea for a story roughly a decade before it ultimately became the novel which was published. The story was to center on Francis Melarky, a young Hollywood technician who eventually kills his mother. Fitzgerald was grimly fascinated by the Leopold and Loeb murders in Chicago and wanted to experiment with the idea of cold-blooded killing.

Melarky, in the course of his travels, encounters a couple, Seth and Diana Piper, and their friend Abe Grant. Later versions of the story take the action away from Melarky and place it on the two males, Seth Piper and Abe Grant. The Pipers become, of course, the Divers, and Abe Grant evolves into Abe North.

An early version of the novel, now mainly about Dick Diver, appeared in *Scribner's Magazine* in 1934, and the novel, revised again, finally appeared as a book later that year. It is this book version, the only full-length rendition of the text to appear in F. Scott Fitzgerald's lifetime, that the following study guide will use as its source.

The difficulty of the Rosemary Hoyt section appearing initially in the novel bothered Fitzgerald in his own lifetime, and, perhaps because the work had not been a financial success and the author hoped that by reworking it, he could improve it, he suggested a re-arrangement of the text to a publisher (Modern Library), but it never appeared.

In 1951 this suggested revision of the novel was edited by Malcolm Cowley and published by Scribner's. The changes that Fitzgerald had listed on the cover of a copy of the novel are the ones that Cowley attempted to put into effect. The 1951 version shifts most of Book 2 to the beginning, to be followed by portions of Book 1. It also would have deleted the section about the Diver visit to the Minghetti's.

Cowley decided not to delete the sections that Fitzgerald recommended, so, in a sense, even the 1951 version is not what the author seems to have recommended. The truth probably is, however, that Fitzgerald's suggestions for changes were themselves never complete, since the dropping of the episodes he suggests leaves gaps in the narrative. The novel, then, is still in a sense incomplete, for had we known Fitzgerald's full wish, the text would probably read differently from either the 1934 or 1951 versions.

The major rearrangement of the text is as follows:

1951 Cowley Version		*1934 Version*
Book I – Case History	=	Chaps. i-ix of Book 2
Book II – Rosemary's Angle	=	Chap. x of Book 2
		Chaps. i-xii of Book 1
Book III – Casualties	=	Chap. xiii-xxv of Book 1
		Chap. xi-xii of Book 2
		– final ¶ "In November"
Book IV – Escape	=	final ¶ of Chap. xii of Book 2
		+ Chap. xiii-xxiii of Book 2
Book V – The Way Home	=	Book 3

Commentaries

BOOK 1

After this novel's original publication, Fitzgerald suggested a reorganization which would have been ordered chronologically and would thus have moved this section farther into the book. The power of the Rosemary Hoyt perception, however, is undeniable, despite the fact that many critics have agreed with Fitzgerald that Rosemary Hoyt, while an interesting character and functional in the narrative, is by no means central, and that beginning with her only misleads the reader into thinking that she will constitute an important segment of the book. Fitzgerald had hoped to publish a version which would have placed the initial chapters of Book 2, which contain Dick Diver's history, as the opening of the novel.

It can easily be argued, however, that this first published version is preferable and that Fitzgerald's first conception of the action was correct. Rosemary Hoyt introduces us less to herself than to the other characters; it is through her eyes that the reader first perceives the action, and as a medium Rosemary is perfect. She is in many ways an innocent: she is but seventeen years old, she has been famous for only six months because of the success of her first movie, *Daddy's Girl*, and, in addition, she is an American and therefore presumably a bit ingenuous and far more trustworthy than a sophisticated European. So the effect of having the Divers' complexity dawn gradually on her is like easing into the Mediterranean setting; we, as readers, can identify with Rosemary more easily than with an impersonal narrator, since we too are as yet uninitiated into the complications of the novel.

Rosemary Hoyt's observations are filtered through her own naïveté. Little knowing how important the Divers will become to her, she and her mother, Elsie Speers, arrive at the Riviera off-season and expect to stay there only three days. We are slowly introduced to the characters of the novel when Rosemary goes down to the beach in front of the hotel where she and her mother have registered. She observes from a distance — both a psychological one, since she is not involved with them, and a physical one, since she belongs to no clique. It is a peculiar lineup of people with their own social geography: one set is obviously established, for they are tanned and comfortable and sit drinking and gossiping under large beach umbrellas. The other group is pale (a sign that they are *arrivistes* and could not have been there very long), sit under ordinary parasols, and are located well back from the sea, where the sand is still filled with gravel and debris. It is the unestablished group which approaches Rosemary, rather like autograph seekers, and thus we are first introduced, via the young actress, to the least important characters of the novel, the defensive McKiscos, a couple of homosexuals (Luis Campion and Royal Dumphrey), and a cheerful elderly lady, Mrs. Abrams. This is a boring, bickering set, and Rosemary is wise in trying to put some distance between them and herself.

Rosemary Hoyt's perception is again faultless when she picks out the leader of the established set as a man in a jockey cap who is, while he entertains his friends, carefully raking the sand and clearing the beach. He seems to be the center of the group less because he talks a lot or shows off but rather because everyone seems to refer things to him, and his quiet cheer seems to constitute the matrix of his party. As in many cases in this novel, this actual event has a basis in F. Scott Fitzgerald's own history: Gerald Murphy, to whom with his wife, Sara, the book is dedicated, did indeed endeavor to clear the beach in front of the Riviera hotel that stayed open in the summer as a courtesy for him and his friends.

Dick Diver, the man in the jockey cap, has caught Rosemary's eye, but he is enigmatic to her, just as in some ways he is for the reader. He is courteous, though aloof. When he awakens Rosemary, after she has been sleeping on the beach and getting sunburned, she would like to converse with him because she finds him attractive. He, however, politely puts away his beach cleaning tools and departs.

Perhaps it is again a mark of Rosemary's innocence and youth that she still believes in love at first sight, for, back at the hotel at lunch, she hints to her mother a bit facetiously that she has fallen in love, almost not understanding that she has done just that. We are to feel Dick Diver's immense magnetism through Rosemary. He is so attractive that she is already in love.

The question that the reader must ask is whether Rosemary can be trusted, whether our first sight of the hero, for example, would have been so unquestioning. The answer can only be stated in artistic terms, for the presence of an intermediary narrator gives texture; one has to become concerned with at least two sets of problems — what is going on and who is witnessing it. The opening chapter sets up, then, two parallel chronicles, that of Dick Diver and that of the woman he will love, Rosemary Hoyt. Just as *Tender is the Night* examines Dick Diver's eventual fall from good fortune, so it witnesses Rosemary's loss of innocence, in nearly every meaning of the word.

The Hollywood ingenue encounters, in the persons of Dick and Nicole Diver, "the exact furthermost evolution of a class." It is a somewhat Jamesian theme, the confrontation between complex and simple, and between old and new. But, whereas Henry James often pitted an American innocent against a more worldly, civilized, and often sinister European, Fitzgerald is working primarily with Americans. Nicole Warren Diver is representative of the new, wealthy, brutal America, for the Warrens are from Chicago, calling to mind the brawling industrial center portrayed so vividly by such writers as Theodore Dreiser and James Farrell. Dick Diver symbolizes the older, established families of Virginia, which, like Fitzgerald's own paternal heritage, ran long on tradition and often short on cash. The two Divers, then, are from diverse backgrounds, and, moreover, they are transplanted or, as it were, Europeanized Americans, adding to their complexity even further. They have created a beautiful life on the Riviera in the south of France, where they have persuaded the owner of Gausse's Hotel to stay open in the summer to accommodate their friends. Customarily, in summer, the upper Riviera, around Deauville, was the center of tourist interest, so the Divers' portion of the sun is, in effect, a retreat. They have built a house, the Villa Diana, with Nicole's money. The villa is, interestingly enough, reconstructed in part from the smaller houses which were already there, as if to preserve that which was native about the spot. The only new part of the villa is the garden, which has a quality that makes the villa seem a world of its own. Indeed, when Rosemary comes to the Divers' party, she feels not only that her hosts have created a world of their own, but also that theirs must be the very center of the world.

Once again Rosemary is more accurate than she knows. Dick Diver's party certainly functions as a way for us (and Rosemary) to get to know the characters. But it also is at once a celebration of Rosemary's growing up and an initiation into the larger world, since it is at the party that she discovers how passionately she loves Dick and also begins to suspect the mystery behind him. But if the Villa Diana is the center of the world, the world is balanced on a rumbling volcano, for the events at the party begin to suggest the history behind the Divers.

Our first extended look at Dick Diver occurs during the party which he gives for all the people on the beach. Here, as before, Dick seems to be the integrator of others, the matrix of the group, the host with social ease and generous impulses. Just as he can bring out an individual's best self by his attentiveness and carefully placed verbal encouragement, so is he able to cohere the diverse factions that have gathered at his home. All the people, except Albert McKisco, who is hopelessly egocentric and aggressive in every conversational attempt, become quite engaged in each other and bask in the glow of Dick's presence.

Not only is the party important to us because Rosemary proclaims her love, and Dick Diver's magic is revealed, but it is crucial to the novel's movement as well. The mystery of what Violet McKisco saw in the bathroom is before us. Had Fitzgerald rearranged the novel as he later desired, he would have sacrificed the dramatic energy of the early mystery. One would be sorry to see the interest lessened by placing this scene later in the book, for it sets up a functional intrigue, the unfolding of which is actually the history of the Divers.

The duel is the first manifestation of that intrigue, since it seems that Tommy Barban is defending the honor of Nicole Diver against the onslaughts of Violet and Albert McKisco. Fitzgerald does a superb job of supplying mystery by not providing explanations in this first book of the novel. The reader learns about the duel from Rosemary, who learns from Campion only that there will be a duel and then, finally, she hears a more complete version from Abe North. An exhausted Abe North is to be McKisco's second because the night before, on the way home from the Divers' party, Violet McKisco had attempted to relate what she saw in the bathroom; Tommy Barban, obviously protecting the Divers in some way, tells her to be quiet before she has a chance to describe the sight; McKisco's response is to challenge Barban to a duel in order to preserve his wife's honor.

So perfectly are we seeing the story through Rosemary's eyes that not only do we not understand why essentially the duel is being fought, but we see the confrontation itself from the sidelines, where she and Campion have secreted themselves. The duel itself is an amusing example of inverted chivalry, for a duel is at least an anachronism, a way of settling an issue which depended for its continuance on such ideals as female honor. McKisco does not really want to fight; he is the least likely candidate for a bloody defense of someone's honor, but he knows that his wife will not forgive him if he does not sustain his challenge, and, melodramatically, he stays up all night putting the finishing touches on his novel, as if he were putting pen to paper for the last time. The duel is a travesty of honor, for once at the site, McKisco, drunk and shaking, is observed not by ranks of chivalric-minded men, but rather by a woman — Rosemary Hoyt — and a homosexual — Luis Campion, who faints at the suggestion of violence. The exchange of shots injures neither party, so the duel is a charade.

But the scene does provide an introductory look at Tommy Barban, whose finely honed sense of violence makes him propose such crude encounters as this, armed with his own magnificent dueling pistols. There is, as well, a peculiar male sense of honor which is not altogether a charade. Although Fitzgerald once described *Tender is the Night* as a "woman's book," the many references to violence, war, and, here, the duel, are telling ones. McKisco is overwhelmed with a sense of pride at his "conquest" in the duel as he staggers off the field. Fitzgerald, seemingly without a sense of irony, says later in the book that the duel was the basis of McKisco's eventual success, since it gave him a basis for self-respect. It is a self-respect cheaply earned, of course, for only a shallow character could purchase pride so easily.

Rosemary Hoyt is perceptive enough to sense the hollow honor in McKisco and to scorn it; she is suddenly seized with laughter after the duel. But it is Dick Diver's seeming completeness that overwhelms her, and with him she has no controlling reservations. His magnetism draws her with the Divers on their trip to Paris.

It is often through seemingly desultory conversation that this novel reveals some interesting insights into its characters. As the scene unfolds in Paris in Chapter xii, for example, one should be aware that Fitzgerald is trying to portray Dick's personality as he sits in restaurants or cafes. As the party sits waiting to be served, for example, they are testing Dick's claim that he is the only American male in the restaurant who has repose, and as various men enter, each exhibits a tic or a physical quirk to reveal underlying tension. His repose is a clue to the Dick Diver personality at its height, and the gentle solidity which informs his relaxed demeanor is the reason women love him and men admire him. His sense of order is paramount, and his active mind encircles everyone with whom he converses. The women who surround him are parasites to the host of his strength, because they are, Fitzgerald says, women who "were all happy to exist in a man's world," dependent for their strength on another. This unquestioned strength of Dick's which seems to engender dependency from others is a theme which appears again and again and will be examined more thoroughly later.

It would be a mistake, however, to paint Dick merely as a broad-minded and secure individual whose history will constitute the book. Fitzgerald has freighted this character with symbolic values that should not be overlooked. One of the author's favorite books at the time was Oswald Spengler's *Decline and Fall of the West*, a fatalistic reading of history which examines the rise and fall of great civilizations. Fitzgerald tries, by showing Dick Diver's sense of history and by exploiting his past to give breadth to his character, to enlarge his hero to become somehow representative of an age, a symbol of completeness which is subject to decay. It would be an error to say that Dick Diver is a twentieth-century Everyman, but it is undeniable that Dick's sense of the past and of his own postwar existence makes him typical, so his fall, therefore, is not simply the fall of a single man, but of a man who might have succeeded in another time.

Dick's preoccupation with the historical past is first revealed in Chapter xiii, when he and Nicole, Rosemary, and the Norths visit the battlefields of World War I. There, in the trenches, he gives the party a running commentary of the battle, then asserts that the war was a "love battle." The phrase strikes us oddly, since war is usually associated with violence, death, and horror. But Dick insists that only the most profound love of one's country would have made men do what they did in that place. By love of country he does not mean a theoretical patriotism mouthed by politicians; he means that only individuals in love with the minute, local romance of everyday life would have had enough spirit to try to defend their homes — this, the case on both sides, explains the intensity of the fight and the desire for victory. The combatants were fighting for their memories, memories it took civilization centuries to construct. In a sense, the disintegration of those memories and dreams was what the war meant; the shattered world could never put itself quite together again. Because Dick understands this fact so deeply and feels civilization's gradual disintegration so keenly, he becomes representative of that decline. As the novel progresses, the reader will see that just as the war haunts Dick because it exploded the values of the modern world, so does the Civil War recur as a kind of refrain to him.

Rosemary Hoyt is so drawn to Dick's compelling presence at the battlefield, so moved by his taking care of a lost woman looking for her brother's grave, so impressed by his being a doctor (which he reveals in the taxi after dinner) that, when they return to their hotel, she offers herself to him. It is a simple and pure act, an example of honest love, freely given, but to her chagrin, Dick refuses her offer. Perhaps this is the beginning of Rosemary's worldly wisdom, for she soon realizes that a beautiful body and untarnished sexual impulses are not enough to conquer Dick Diver. At the height of his self-assuredness and mature self-respect, Dick is able to say "no" to an affair that would hurt Nicole, destroy Rosemary's virginity, and lower his own self-esteem. It is a decision of simple strength of character that is soon to be eroded.

Rosemary's change has begun. That her frank offer to Dick Diver is in startling contrast to her earlier self is revealed by her movie. In Paris she arranges to have a private showing of her immensely popular film, *Daddy's Girl*, and, on the screen, the party sees the original, saccharine-sweet Rosemary, before whose tiny fist the forces of lust and corruption rolled away." It is an example of the Shirley Temple type of child beauty that Americans fell in love with for a while. Such simplicity has a sinister side, of course, because however much one might wish that simple beauty and virtue would triumph, they rarely do in the real world. The "Daddy's Girl" theme, moreover, has its dark Freudian underside that makes Dick, and all present-day readers with him, flinch—the theme of incest. In a sense, the phrase "Daddy's Girl" is the catchword for all the females in the book; at this point in the novel, however, it is the foreshadowing of the Nicole Diver mystery soon to be unfolded.

Rosemary, however, currently retains some of her film screen "innocence," for she wants to give Dick a screen test so that someday he can perhaps come to Hollywood and be her "leading man"—that is, her "daddy." Again, Dick refuses, but Rosemary's beauty has begun to work on him, and the first crack in his character has begun to show. Rosemary's tenacity finally conquers, for, having taken her to a party given by some ambitious and "arty" Americans, he finally acknowledges his love for her during the taxi ride home.

Another hint of the less-than-innocent Rosemary Hoyt comes in the person of Collis Clay, who has joined the party in Paris. Collis is a Yale student who dated Rosemary in America. He seems good-natured and uncomplicated, content to be near his vision of loveliness, since it is clear that Rosemary is not in love with him. His objectivity about Rosemary comes to haunt Dick, however, since be begins, during a conversation in a cafe to tell him about an episode on a train the previous year. Rosemary and Hillis, an acquaintance of Collis from New Haven, desiring to be alone in their train compartment, locked the door and closed the curtain, an act which the train conductor viewed as an impropriety, since the two were not married. An argument ensued, which Collis was able to stop, but the scene haunts Dick, and the suspicion that Rosemary is not a virgin recurs to Dick as a kind of refrain:

—Do you mind if I pull down the curtain?
—Please do. It's too light in here.

Collis Clay is a walk-on character; he seems to be introduced and to be paraded whenever Fitzgerald wants to purvey some information—in this case, the suggestion that Dick has not perceived Rosemary correctly and also the suggestion that goodness is not always what it seems. With the Collis Clay episode, as well, the novel passes out of Rosemary's voice, since she, as a perceptor, has outworn her usefulness.

Until this point in the novel, Nicole Diver has been seen only fleetingly. One knows little about her except that she is very beautiful and has a deep love for Dick, an example of which occurs in a whispered conversation (Chapter xii) which Rosemary overhears while she is in a phone booth making a call. The

Divers set an assignation later at the hotel, an act which has all the passion and freshness of young, unmarried, even illicit love; Rosemary envies this quality of amorousness. Again, during a shopping trip with Rosemary, a bit more information is revealed when Nicole sees the hotel in Paris where she stayed during her teens. Nicole, though American, has lived in Europe much of her life. These are the only bits of information that Rosemary has garnered about Nicole.

Largely because Rosemary is also in love with Dick and cannot, therefore, view Nicole completely, Fitzgerald changes his narrative perspective in Chapter xix, excluding Rosemary from the major action. In the preceding chapters the actress has not actually narrated the action, but the reader has the feeling that she is present and that the author is trying to recount events as she would have seen them. Both to proceed with the action and to strengthen the character of Nicole, several scenes follow which are narrated impersonally.

There are some early clues to Nicole's nature in the scene with Abe North in the Gare Saint Lazare. Abe North, the debilitated and alcoholic musician and composer, is supposed to leave Paris by train, and he has asked Nicole to come early to be with him. The dissipated musician wants, we suspect, to confess his love to Nicole, but he is unable to do so; finally he says that he is "tired of women's worlds." It is an obscure comment for most readers. Abe probably means that women are continually integrating things and that Abe, because he is an artist, must explode or even destroy things to discover newness. Almost immediately after his comment, a woman quite literally destroys something, however, for she shoots a man down.

At this point it would be fair to say that Fitzgerald wants us to think that in women's worlds, men succumb. The murderess was Maria Wallis, an acquaintance of the Divers; in fact, Nicole had just spoken with her shortly before the shooting. Her victim is an Englishman, presumably her lover. It is a startling and grim metaphor for the future of the male/female relationships during the rest of the novel.

Equally as chilling is Nicole's response to the event. Dick, in what we can presume to be a typical, concerned action, is about to follow Maria to the police station to secure her release and to help her, when Nicole intervenes with a curt comment that the best—and only—thing to do is to phone Maria's sister and let her manage it. Nicole is suddenly revealed not only as being sensible, but, more significantly, as having power over Dick. The party leaves the Gare Saint Lazare (where, like Lazarus, men die and rise again), the violence echoing within them.

In a certain sense, *Tender is the Night* is the great book of sadness that it is because it is a novel about endings—farewells, death, disintegration, and a falling from honor. The episodes following Chapter xxii are particularly representative of this continual leave-taking, since here Fitzgerald seems to introduce new characters only to have them swept off the stage.

Abe North who, the morning of the previous day was supposed to have left Paris for America, did not actually leave. He returned to Paris, a fact unknown to the Divers, and drank all night. Though Fitzgerald supplies few facts, apparently there had been a quarrel in which Abe North thought he was being robbed; he accused a black man, and the police (mistakenly, it is revealed) jail a Negro restaurateur, a Mr. Freeman. The ironies abound. The name Abe North is redolent of all the racial tension of the South, both before and after the Civil War. In one of the earlier versions of *Tender,* Abe appeared as "Abe Grant," so the complex of the Northern white man becomes, in a sense, Abraham Lincoln/Ulysses S. Grant/ and the North. This same (composite) person is responsible for the unjust arrest of a "free man," which, of course, the black man would always have been had it not been for the white man. In addition, Abe calls the Divers to tell them of his mistake and to indicate that he hopes the trouble will be solved by another black emissary, a Jules Peterson who witnessed the "crime." Mr. Peterson manufactures shoe polish; the fact that the shoe shine boy has typically been black, linked with the fact that Jules Peterson is from Scandinavia, which we associate with blonds, compounds the irony: a free man, having been jailed by the freedom-bestowing North, is to be freed by a black man who wants to be free of his blackness by *manu-facturing* shoe polish in a land of blonds.

When Peterson goes into the hall to wait until Rosemary and the Divers have been able to talk to Abe North, he is punished for his complicity with the whites (and all white America, represented by Abe North): when Rosemary returns to her room, she finds Peterson, murdered, lying across her bed. Other black men, originally responsible for the misdeed followed Peterson and, to silence his testimony, murdered him. The misdeed itself comes into question, for acquaintances of Abe North said that the "criminal" was guilty only of taking a fifty-franc note out of Abe's hand to pay for a round of drinks which Mr. North had ordered. A murder has been committed because of a misunderstanding.

The cracks in Dick Diver's personality occurred when he began to make tentative love to Rosemary. His submission to Nicole's suggestion about Maria Wallis is a second clue to his possible demise. The third clue to Dick Diver's disintegration comes at the end of Book 1, when, in an attempt to save Rosemary's honor, he removes the corpse from her bed and places it in the hall, changes the sheets, then calmly calls the hotel manager to report an unfortunate murder victim in the hall, extracting from the manager the promise that the matter will be handled discreetly, both for his sake and for the establishment's.

On the one hand, we observe the courteous and insightful Dick Diver, for he is quick to realize the implications of the crime and he knows that Rosemary's career would be ruined if her name were linked in any way to the murder of a black man; thus he acts quickly to save her. But it is a morally ambiguous act. Is Rosemary's so-called honor worth saving? And the fact remains that a man has been murdered. The crime will never be sufficiently investigated because the Divers and Abe North will never tell the truth. The scene is a dramatic comment on moral complexity; no act is simple, and Dick Diver, who earlier seemed to be a paragon of responsibility and virtue, leaves the last scene with his hands stained.

When we finish Book 1, Fitzgerald has suggested to us many of Dick Diver's future difficulties. In the final scene, Rosemary sees the sight which Violet McKisco witnessed earlier: Nicole is swaying madly beside the bathtub, talking incoherently, and accusing Dick. Rosemary now knows the Divers' secret—that Nicole has periods of madness. Book 1 comes full circle, ending with Rosemary's perception, as it began with her observations on the beach in front of Gausse's Hotel. The difference now is that the mystery is out, and the rest of the novel will be an exposition of how the Divers came to be where they are and what will happen to them from that point.

BOOK 2

Chapters i-x

The first ten chapters of this section establish the chronological background for Book 1, and it is in this portion of the novel that the reader at last begins to understand the complicated history behind the Divers' facade of pure and simple marital love; here is a more complete unfolding of the mysterious scene in the bathroom witnessed by Violet McKisco in Chapter vii and by Rosemary Hoyt in Chapter xxv of Book 1.

It is necessary to briefly summarize Dick Diver's past in order to understand how Fitzgerald is trying to create his hero. The period before Dick's marriage to Nicole had seemed to be a "heroic period," for this was the time of his youth when he was a promising young psychiatrist. His credentials for success seemed unassailable—an education at Yale, a year as a Rhodes scholar in Oxford, a degree from Johns Hopkins University, and, starting in 1917, an interval in Zurich which would yield a degree and a book, published in 1920, a work which was to become a standard textbook in the field of psychiatry. His climb to success has been filled with good fortune. Fitzgerald describes Dick as the "complete hero," a man who has had every advantage and has succeeded. He is the Western man whose destiny is the fall from good fortune, just as the destiny of the Western world seems to be disintegration after the great "love war" of 1914-18. The only way Dick Diver can go is "down" (indeed, his very name is a clue to his spiral descent), for his position in the world has been postulated on his own seemingly infallible strength and reason, on the world's beneficence, and "the lies of generations of frontier mothers who had to croon falsely, that there were no wolves outside the cabin door." The frontier metaphor is especially appropriate here, for the bravery of early Americans has made the generation of Dick Divers possible.

At twenty-nine, Dick Diver might have been, Fitzgerald says, like Grant in Galena, a metaphor from the Civil War which needs explaining. After eleven years in the U.S. Army, Ulysses S. Grant was asked to resign because of a severe drinking problem. He spent the time before he was recalled for the Civil War as a clerk in a leather goods store in Galena, Illinois; he was called to duty in 1861 and embarked on a course which was to catapult him to leadership of the Northern armies, to the defeat of the Confederate cause, and, eventually, to the presidency of the United States. The author means by the metaphor that the creative lull between two periods of greatness is what Dick Diver thought was his condition. His past, while satisfactory and full of promise, should have been but a prelude to a distinguished future. But the Dick Diver whose story we are reading is not to have the success that Grant did as a general.

Dick Diver's history at this point includes Nicole, and if Dick's past is full of promise and distinction, Nicole's is just the opposite. It is from the comparison of the two lives that are to merge that the reader first sees how the novel is to embody the principle of transference: Dick and Nicole start at opposite corners of a rectangle — she at the low side, he on the high. And as Dick's line goes down, Nicole's rises. Just as Dick Diver begins his adult life whole and full of hope, Nicole starts hers as a shattered and empty woman.

Nicole's plight is revealed by a conversation in Chapter ii between Dick and Franz Gregorovius of the Dohmler Clinic; Dick has been consulted on the case of a young woman, and her illness is being discussed as the two doctors travel toward the clinic in Zurich. The patient in question is Nicole Warren, daughter of a wealthy Chicago industrialist; Nicole's mother died when Nicole was eleven years old. Her father brought his daughter to the clinic for help because she wasn't "right in the head." Doctor Dohmler's subsequent interviews with the father had revealed a case of incest. And, while there was a seeming normalcy for many years, it is now clear that this initiation into sex presumably scarred her for life.

Dick Diver was early drawn to Nicole, before he even knew that she was a patient, because of her beauty. This is a sinister fact, for it suggests that Dick, wooed by her physical sensuousness will be out of intellectual control when he deals with her. After their initial acquaintance, the young woman writes letters to Dick, in which the principle of transference begins to work, since she begins placing herself and her problems in someone else's hands. It should be noted, by the way, that many portions of these letters were taken from letters which Zelda Fitzgerald wrote her husband during her stay in a mental hospital in Switzerland, and she had called Scott, in some of her letters, "Mon Capitaine," just as Nicole does. Zelda's problem, of course, was not incest but rather, at the time of her hospitalization, incipient schizophrenia. Fitzgerald believed rather firmly in transference, however, and he knew the spiritual exhaustion of his having to minister to Zelda's moods.

That F. Scott Fitzgerald rather mercilessly mined his own wife's illness for his novel could account for the particular poignancy of these scenes in Zurich. Dick Diver seems to fall in love nearly against his will, almost as Fitzgerald wanted to exonerate himself from any guilt about Zelda's illness by suggesting that he was trapped into his relationship with his wife.

The lovers' meeting in Chapter v is especially important not only because it amplifies Dick and Nicole's new love but also because it sheds some meaning on the title of the novel. Nicole takes Dick to a secret place on the grounds of the sanitarium in order to listen to some American records she has smuggled in. There in the dark and quiet they listen to the tunes and,

Fitzgerald says, between songs "a cricket held the scene together with a single note." The cricket in this scene functions much the way the nightingale does in Keats's "Ode to a Nightingale," a phrase of which gave the title to Fitzgerald's novel. In both instances the song of the creature is simple and repetitive, which gives human beings feelings of everlastingness. The lovers in *Tender is the Night* and the poet in "Ode to a Nightingale" seem placed at some remove from reality, and that isolation does, for a moment, make the subjects think of the fleeting moment as lasting forever.

Dick's love for Nicole Warren creates a conflict for him, but, in addition, it creates problems for the other professionals, Doctor Dohmler and Franz Gregorovius, who frankly tell Dick that his getting too personal with Nicole could spoil the chances of successfully treating her. Dick, however, cannot keep himself from responding to the youth and beauty of the patient, although his professional self realizes that if Nicole's so-called "transference" becomes love, he could be creating problems for both of them. When he makes the break with Nicole, Dick is torn, because while he does what he thinks is professionally responsible, he is touched by his infatuation with the woman. At this time in his rather charmed life, however, Dick Diver is still a man of some psychological strength, and he is able to part with her, though he knows how it hurts them both.

The sound of doom is relentless, however, and they must meet again. During the period of their breakup Dick had begun his second book, the same book that he will work on throughout their marriage and never finish. It is probably no mistake on Fitzgerald's part that the rising of Nicole's star in Dick Diver's life is accompanied by the setting of the psychologist's own professional star. The surprising thing about such a writer as Fitzgerald, whom one associates with the *joie de vivre* of the twenties in America, is a deep-seated, almost puritanical attitude about the value of work. Dick Diver's greatest satisfaction lies in working well, and once he begins to lag in his work, his value as an integrated human being begins to erode.

Even though Dick has thrown himself into his professional research with a will, he is diverted again by Nicole, this time by a chance. In Chapter viii Dick is energetically making a bicycling trip up the mountains. There, having taken the funicular rail car to the top, he encounters Nicole and a young Italian (Marmora), and Dick, determined not to join the merry couple, retires to a different hotel.

After dinner Dick meets not only Nicole, but her older sister, Baby Warren, certainly one of Fitzgerald's most startling fictional creations. Her name, Baby, is possibly drawn from real life, since Zelda's family nickname was "Baby" because she was the last, and in many ways, the favored child of Judge and Mrs. Sayre. Baby Warren has very little that is infantile about her, though some critics say that she is still in the egocentric, thus infantile, stage of emotional development. Her name becomes more sinister, however, if it is viewed as an ironic inversion. Far from being innocent, she is shrewd and calculating about her finances and she feels assured of her ability to manipulate people by buying them off. In addition to being a calculating and wealthy female, she is unmarried and likely to remain so, and, in some ways, Fitzgerald means this fact to be damning, for from her sexual inflexibility is born her lack of submissiveness, or, if one wants to interpret it that way, her lack of femininity. He refers to her as slightly "onanistic," an interesting adjective not only because of its suggestion of non-productivity and egoism, but also because it usually refers to male, rather than female, masturbatory practices.

Baby Warren is clearly concerned about her sister and wants to protect her, but her solution, as explained to Dick Diver in Chapter ix, is to purchase Nicole's emotional security by "buying" her a doctor. Mr. Warren, Baby explains, has given much money to the University of Chicago, and certainly it would be possible to get Nicole into the university crowd, where a professor would surely, for her financial attractiveness, want to marry her.

Ironically, Baby Warren's idea of a protector for Nicole comes to pass, for Dick finally decides that he loves, and wants to marry, his former mental patient. There is no indication that Baby Warren ever knew the real cause of her sister's problem, so she certainly would not have perceived that in many ways Nicole was making a "daddy" of her new husband. She disapproves of the match, but not, therefore, for the right reasons. Her attitude is that Dick's background is poor and commonplace, so the alliance is undesirable; when she asks about his origins, Dick tells her that he is a direct descendant of Mad Anthony Wayne, and Baby, in her historical ignorance, replies that there is already quite enough madness in the whole affair. Wayne, a Revolutionary War hero and Indian fighter, was called "mad" only because of his cool-headed military brilliance which manifested itself in seemingly insane maneuvers that usually resulted in victory. Dick would like to ally himself with such calculated madness as he proposes his own mad scheme — marrying a mental patient.

The last section of Chapter x is a monologue by Nicole, and it consists of jumbled sections of either conversation or mental wanderings. It is the only time in the book when Nicole is allowed her own voice, so it deserves examination. It summarizes the history of the marriage from its inception, through the birth of two children, through marginal insanity, to, at last, her perception of Rosemary Hoyt on the beach. While it has taken some fifty pages to sketch in Dick's history, Nicole's years since her hospitalization are covered in this concise and poetic few pages.

Her comments are characterized first by a lack of concern about money, and she indicates that Dick refuses to share her wealth: it is really a burden to them both. Her refusal to think about her money, however, results in her spending it thoughtlessly, a situation Dick will find difficult.

The births of the two children seem to be interludes of near insanity. During her first hospitalization she saw a lady who gave birth to a "blue baby," who died. Such a situation, however, might threaten even the stability of a normal pregnant woman. Nonetheless, the arrival of Lanier, the first child, seems to be followed by traveling for her health, for she mentions singing

nonsense songs near the lifeboats, while people in the deck
chairs stare. There has been some mental recovery after the trips,
which seem to have taken them as far as Africa. Then their second child, Topsy, is born, and, she says, "everything got dark
again." There is an especially significant sentence after the
Topsy reference, when Nicole says, "I want to be a fine person
like you, Dick—I would study medicine except it's too late."
Fitzgerald probably is trying to indicate the extent of character
identity the two have, for later in the book it becomes clear that
Nicole has no sense of self except for her identification with
Dick; so completely dependent is she on him that she wants
actually to *be* him, even to the extent of copying his profession.
Fitzgerald himself was especially unreceptive to any of Zelda's
attempts at a career for herself, but he became particularly dis-
tressed when she attempted to write, perhaps because he considered it an infringement on his profession. This sentence, at
least, seems to indicate that Nicole's desire to be like her husband was rooted in sickness, and one cannot help wondering
whether that was Fitzgerald's attitude toward his own wife's
literary efforts.

In the last section of Nicole's soliloquy, she wishes for a
larger dwelling for the now enlarged family. That fact, joined
with Dick's desire for a place where he can work and amplified
by their mutual desire to be "brown and young" in the sun, result in their purchasing property on the Riviera. The last sen-
tences show her if not actually happy, at least content and
domestic. She sits translating a recipe for Chicken Maryland into
French, the activity which Rosemary Hoyt first saw her involved
in. The concluding sentence is a fine transition into the next
section of the novel, where Nicole will lose herself again, this
time because of Rosemary.

BOOK 2

Chapters xi-xxiii

Nearly midway in Book 2, events take up roughly where
they left off at the end of Book 1, but now there is an added

tension—Nicole's mental illness. The calm has been shattered by Rosemary's seeing Nicole in the bathroom, babbling insanely. The reader has also been given a case history, as it were, in the first half of Book 2. This history has been presented in two voices—first, from the vantage point of authorial omniscience which, one assumes, explains the truth in objective terms, and, second, from Nicole's sometimes deranged point of view which, while covering the historical events, also adds the dramatic dimension of her uncertain mental state.

In the remainder of Book 2, events center on Dick Diver; the narrator follows him as he begins to perceive his situation and even to yield to it. Dick's decisiveness becomes progressively eroded, and his actions become a moral shadowboxing, for his struggle revealed here, shows him trying to save himself (*not* Nicole and *not* Rosemary) and finally realizing that he will fail.

Dick Diver's chief moral burden is, of course, his love for Nicole, because he increasingly realizes that he is her doctor as well as her husband, and after each of her breakdowns he must labor to put her back together again. It has also become clear to Dick that maintaining a financial independence is difficult. Fitzgerald describes Dick as an ascetic; he requires a few worldly goods to survive. After his marriage, for example, when he travels he always stays in economy hotels and drinks cheap wine. But Nicole's wealth, almost insidiously, begins to surround him; the magnificence of the Villa Diana, the Divers' house on the Riviera, is inescapable, and their entire life-style is set by Nicole's money. It would, however, be too facile to say that Dick's tragic flaw, the weakness which inexorably spells doom for him, is his succumbing to wealth. He is a much more complicated character than that; the fact of financial plenty, however, does erode his ability to work, which in turn drains his own self-esteem.

The crucial fact in Dick's decline is not really Nicole or her money, though both are contributing factors. It is, rather, his realization that he is in love with Rosemary. His feeling is revealed in a conversation with Elsie Speers, Rosemary's mother, in Chapter xi, though the verbalization of his infatuation with Rosemary surprises him more than it does Mrs. Speers. To the tension of dealing with the sick Nicole and the well Nicole is added, then, the complicating factor of a new love.

Dick is quite aware that for Nicole's sanity and his own peace of mind, he must exorcise Rosemary's spirit. Nicole already seems to understand Dick's new attachment, and she seems to goad him into conversation about her. Perhaps it is but testimony to Dick's weakness that an emotional abyss is created by his cold and professional attention to Nicole; the warmth of love for Rosemary threatens to fill that void.

In Chapter xii Dick perceives his entrapment: he is entrapped by Nicole's wealth, his own diminished ability to work, and his love for Rosemary. As he sits down to play "Tea for Two" at the piano, he suddenly knows that Nicole will hear it and guess, quite correctly, that the "two" in Dick's heart are himself and Rosemary. A quality of constraint is forced upon his life.

The weakening of his resolve is best typified by his submission to the Warren money in the purchase of a clinic. In Chapter xiii, Dick Diver struggles to maintain his own dignified independence, but his opponents are strong. The scene is Gstaad, Switzerland, a ski resort where Fitzgerald himself with his daughter, Scottie, vacationed briefly to restore themselves after Zelda's admission to the Prangins Clinic. Nicole has once again recovered, but Dick lives with the sinister threat of a recurrence of her illness ever ominous. So when Franz Gregorovius, his former working partner at Zurich, approaches him with the proposal that they buy a clinic and undertake to manage it together, he should be delighted: it would be a means of committing himself once again to his career by practicing on a day-to-day basis with patients. Almost immediately it becomes clear, however, that Franz is approaching him not because of his professional qualifications but because of his having easily accessible money for capital.

When Dick cynically brings Baby Warren into the conversation, the reader understands that Dick Diver realizes — with pain — that he is once more to be "purchased." Baby Warren was able to buy a doctor for Nicole; now she wants to buy a clinic for her sister. The author tells us Baby's thoughts at this time — if Nicole lives near a clinic, Baby would never worry about her. Dick's future is sealed.

Dick's utter captivity is revealed on the sleigh trip back to the hotel, when the party includes a young Englishman who regales the company with tales of how a friend and he "love" each other by boxing for an hour. Dick finds the assertion absurd and the young man a bounder; when the young Englishman angrily cuts off the discussion with "If you don't understand, I can't explain it to you," Dick falls silent, admonishing himself by musing, "This is what I'll get if I begin saying what I think." Defeated by the forces of money and responsibility for his wife, Dick decides to open the clinic with Franz. Chapter xiii ends with a lyrical good-bye, another of the novel's poignant leavetakings.

But the clinic, far from spelling professional happiness for Dick and security for Nicole, is but another rung on Dick's professional ladder down. The symbolic clue to Dick's defeat is his dream at the beginning of Chapter xiv. He dreams at first of orderly rows of uniforms marching to the second movement of Prokofiev's *Love for Three Oranges;* but the vision is shattered by fire engines, "symbols of disaster," and an uprising of mutilated war victims. In his notebook Dick describes the dream, then concludes, "non-combatant's shell-shock."

The phrase is important because it again reveals Dick Diver's fascination with war, as his tour of the battlefields did earlier. It should be noted that he is a non-combatant in several senses: while formally in the army in Zurich, he never saw duty; rather, he spent the time completing his degree in psychiatry. He is also an onlooker in the struggles that seem to determine his life: increasingly, Nicole's needs and Baby Warren's bank account dictate his actions. Finally, and not the least important, is the relation to Fitzgerald's own life, when in a spirit of patriotism, he signed up to go to war in 1917 but got only as far as Alabama. But like everyone else in postwar America, Fitzgerald was a victim of the war, though he was a non-combatant.

Dick Diver is, at the clinic, more lonely than ever and more ruled than ever. He has to work full-time at his career and, at the same time, support his wife mentally. At this point in her life, Nicole's only commitment to life is her husband: "When he turned away from her into himself he left her holding Nothing in her hands and staring at it, calling it many names, but knowing it was only the hope that he would come back soon." Yet the feeling is not reciprocal; Dick's life never depended, wholly, on Nicole.

There is a paradox in the dependence relationship which readers can sense — even though Fitzgerald himself did not seem to realize it — perhaps because in a very real sense he was writing about himself and Zelda, and they never were able to understand each other on the question of independence in marriage. On the one hand, Nicole is, and always has been, clinging. By the end of the story, her originally dependent relation to Dick has moved into a kind of independence. The implication in the pattern of transference in the novel is that Nicole feeds off Dick's strength; she is a parasite and he is host, and she grows stronger as he becomes weaker, until she can eventually toss him away. One must assume that Fitzgerald views this dependency as poisonous, since the hero (in many ways Fitzgerald himself) is defeated. He clearly approves of Dick's original ambition in his career and his early strength and independence, so that as he chronicles his fall from strength, Fitzgerald tacitly assumes that independence of body and mind is best.

The character of the "Iron Maiden" in Chapter xiv is what gives the lie to Fitzgerald's real attitude about male/female relations and helps explain why the characterization of Nicole is as confused as it is. The Iron Maiden is a favorite patient of Doctor Diver's; he cares for her deeply and wants to protect her (as he wanted to care for Nicole and as Fitzgerald wanted to help

Zelda). Her plight is that her body is completely covered with eczema, the same painful skin eruption that Zelda Fitzgerald suffered in the Swiss clinic. When Doctor Diver converses with the Iron Maiden (so called because she is clad in her disease as completely as if she was encased in the medieval torture device of spike-lined armor), she says she is "sharing the fate of the women of my time who challenged men to battle." The surface suggestion is that she is dying of syphilis (later Franz, in his dull way, insists that, despite tests, this was the case), but the deeper meaning is that, as in the case of Zelda Fitzgerald, her psychological sickness is a desire to be a man—independent, creative in her own right. That "sickness" is manifested by a painful physical condition. She is, simply, by her physical make-up, not equal to the strain of having her own identity. Women who are not submissive and dependent will, it seems, succumb.

Fitzgerald never seems to understand that to invest one's self completely in another (as he implies that the Iron Maiden should have done) is the reverse side of the Nicole coin. Nicole, by her vampire-like dependence, finally bleeds her husband to powerlessness. We have evidence, then, from the Iron Maiden and Nicole respectively, that independence in women must be bought at a man's expense. The woman who has an identity of her own either will destroy herself—or her man—in the process.

One of Dick Diver's problems is that he realizes that Nicole's dependence is a heavy liability; if the author were to have been consistent, he would have had Nicole maintain her childish dependence to the end and that relationship would have brought her, and Dick, happiness. Since Fitzgerald seems to be saying very clearly that a marriage between two fully independent people is impossible, one could assume that he would approve of a moral unit: the husband and wife are one and act as one.

Later in the book, when Nicole pleads for help and understanding from Dick after her madness at the carnival, he is deeply disturbed by the knowledge that he and Nicole will not be able to succeed together. Here again, Fitzgerald verbalizes his prototypical—and probably destructive—theory about dependency. Men, he says, are "beam and idea, girder and logarithm." Presumably the completed metaphor would make women brick and cement, the practical and concrete expansion of the building. The sexes would thus be complementary and mutually interdependent. Nicole and Dick, in Doctor Diver's mind, will fail because they are "one and equal." They are so involved in each other that they cannot even be divided into interdependency; his destruction, therefore, is carried on at the same time as hers. He cannot see her as broken and suffering without becoming so himself. If Dick Diver's assessment were true, however, Dick would rise at the same time Nicole does—instead of becoming, as he does, the shell of his former self.

Nicole's usurpation of Dick is manifested by her jealousy, first about Rosemary and, second, in Chapter xv, about a former mental patient who writes to say that Dick has seduced her daughter. Nicole believes the woman; Dick, innocent, is impatient with such claims, perhaps not realizing how desperately Nicole needs to own him.

The climax of Nicole's jealousy and madness is examined in the carnival scene in Chapter xv. To have chosen a carnival as the vehicle of madness is a particularly appropriate metaphor. Carnivals originated as popular celebrations of the ecclesiastical calendar, and they were typified by temporary schizophrenia, for, with a mask and costume, the participant could become another person. This duality seems to be part of the human condition, and probably few psychologists would argue that setting aside one celebration a year, where human beings could change identities, is not unconstructive.

Nicole's "carnival," however, lasts longer. Earlier, in Chapter xiv, Nicole is described as being without any identity, save that which she has in Dick. The carnival underscores that condition, for the thought of losing Dick to another is not simple jealousy; it means, quite literally, losing herself. As the family drives along the mountain road toward the festival, Nicole withdraws increasingly. The tension is high. There will have to be an explosion soon, one feels. Once at the carnival, she is described as being disoriented, unable to anchor herself to any object. When at last she begins to run wildly into the crowd, one does not know whether she is fleeing from something or toward something. In the novel there have been three occasions of these mad fits, and they have each occurred after an event which threatened to take Dick away from Nicole — twice because she saw the love he bore for Rosemary and, the last time, because of a letter from a former patient. Nicole becomes literally insane at the thought of losing her husband, who is nothing less than her being.

Fitzgerald describes these scenes powerfully; the reader can feel the confusion and sound of carnival merriment which contrasts so strongly with the very serious chase going on within it. Dick pursues his wife and, at one point, time seems to stand still, for he circles the merry-go-round until he realizes that he is running at the same rate that it is, and he is staring at the same horse. It is a suspension of time reminiscent of the cricket's song earlier in Chapter v.

When Dick finally manages to find Nicole, she is on the ferris wheel, in the top seat, and she laughs hysterically all the way down. The ferris wheel, again, is a most suitable metaphor for Nicole's plight; the wheel turns, inexorably, in a circle and no forward progress is ever gained. But in the rotating motion, the world at least seems to change from the clarity and proximity of the real world, when the chair is at the ground level, to the distance and distortion when the chair is at the top.

As Nicole descends to earth — and perhaps to reality — Dick is able to grab her. Their brief conversation suggests that not only is Nicole suspicious of the former inmate who had written Dick, but also that she has seen a girl in the carnival crowd who, she thinks, was making advances to him. It is hard to determine whether Nicole's jealousy causes her madness or whether her madness causes her jealousy. It does seem, however, that her illness has to do with "daddies" and a fear of being left alone. In addition, she has an acute realization that she is ill, just as Zelda Fitzgerald did.

The climax of Chapter xv is based on a real experience from the Fitzgeralds' life. On their drive home, Nicole reaches over and jerks the steering wheel from Dick, nearly catapulting the car over a cliff. Dick, with difficulty, is able to right the wheels again, but the car veers into some bushes and tips on its side. Zelda did the same thing; her impulse at the time, she said later, was that she was trying to save them, not destroy them. It is interesting to note that Fitzgerald chooses to view Nicole's action as one of evil; Dick wants to smash in her face because he believes she consciously wanted to destroy them all. Dick Diver, as a psychiatrist, should not see this act as malevolence but rather as sickness, a fact which suggests that Dick Diver at this point is also the author: Fitzgerald writes himself into the character so much that it is less Dick Diver thinking of Nicole than F. Scott Fitzgerald who wants to knock some sense into Zelda. Such confusion of self and character often explains seeming inconsistencies in the novel. For the first time in the novel, for example, we are told that Dick Diver must try to keep Nicole away from brandy, both at the carnival and at the inn after the accident. The overtones are that Nicole is an alcoholic as well as a schizophrenic. It seems odd that this rather important fact has not been mentioned before and is not alluded to again in the novel. In real life, of course, it was not Zelda who was addicted to alcohol. Almost as if to make Nicole's illness a composite of all illness, Fitzgerald at this point transfers his own problems into the character of Nicole. Even though Nicole Diver is a triumph of collected weakness and loss of self, she ultimately conquers because so "one and equal" are she and Dick that only one of them can have the identity they share. It is a sick love, this identification of oneself completely with another, oddly like the Catherine/Heathcliff amour so powerfully described by Emily Brontë in *Wuthering Heights*.

Nicole's struggles have already robbed Dick of the self he once had, and in Chapter xvi he sets out to find himself again. He has to leave the clinic and Nicole behind in what is not so much an escape as a search. His travels take him to all the places and people where rescue might lie; he is being led to the desert of his own self where he no longer will be able to find the nourishment of continuance.

Ostensibly attending a psychiatric convention in Berlin, Dick leaves Zurich by plane, feeling that he has "abandoned sickness to the sick, sound to the motors, direction to the pilot." Would that it were so easy to find oneself. He is actually on a sentimental journey, hoping to be led back to his simple roots, where his father preached sermons about what was good and right; then, his only concern, as a boy, was how much money to put in the collection plate. He is looking for the early, simple, and sweet Wordsworthian wholeness of youth in an attempt to find what he is; somewhere, he knows, he has gone astray.

Instead of simple truths, Dick finds corruption, sin, and grime in Munich, his first stop. By chance, he encounters Tommy Barban whom he has not seen since their days on the Riviera. Barban's name is very close to "barbarian," and his brute power and corruption was early suggested both by the duel and by Tommy's career — that of fighting in wars. Tommy Barban, without principle, will fight in anyone's war, and his recent exploits show no reformation. His job apparently had been to free a Russian prince named Chillicheff, who had been in hiding. The rescuers killed three men to free the prince, and Dick Diver, and all sensitive people with him, wonders whether the life of one decaying Russian monarchist is worth that of three young men doing their duty.

Dick's psyche needs healing, but instead it is dealt horror. To senseless killing is added death, the surprise knowledge of Abe North's demise. And not even Abe died a peaceful death; he was "beaten to death in a speakeasy," degradation added to death. The recurring motif of war enters Dick's dreams that night, this time a collection of war veterans going to lay wreaths on the tombs of the dead. It is Dick's paean to Abe whom he had known in earlier and better days.

In Chapter xviii, Dick Diver's hegira continues, but events again conspire tragically. He is alone, he says, "for his soul's sake"; it is an attempt to search within himself and disentangle himself from Nicole's complicated life. Nicole's presence has not only forced Dick to be a full-time on-duty doctor; her money has dictated that his career involve dealing with monied people — both socially and professionally. It is clear that Dick is not really attracted to money itself, as some critics have said, but rather that stacks of cash have begun to obscure his vision. At one point he quietly realizes that he has spent most of his professional life "teaching the rich the ABC's of human decency."

Decency is a key word: decency is not learned; it is a natural charity and understanding of others. The embodiment of this natural courtesy and morality for Dick, of course, has been his father, and as he begins to realize the supreme naturalness of his father's goodness, he begins to yearn for that same facility of living for himself. His desire for the simplicity and innocence of his original self takes two strong paths — one, to the innocence of new love (elaborated on later), and, second, a yearning for the simple life of his American father. Such easy recapture of his original self, however, is impossible. While at a hotel in Innsbruck,, Austria, Dick receives a telegram. It tells him of his father's death.

Whereas many of Fitzgerald's walk-on characters (Collis Clay and Luis Campion) never achieve any stature, the figure of Dick Diver's father is a powerful one, though he is spoken of only briefly and always in Dick's reminiscences. He is a symbol of the cultivated, naturally courteous, older generation which has passed. It is interesting to note that for all F. Scott Fitzgerald's leadership in the "Jazz Age," there is a sense in which he scorned the new values and clung to an older, more rigid conception of the world. Dick's memory of his father comes in a brief flashback, years ago when he was walking downtown with him; Mr. Diver is proud of his son and he tells him brief anecdotes which, like parables, are quiet and effective. The things he learned from his father, Dick realizes, were simple and honest — and accurate.

The book has, as stated earlier, a veritable refrain of farewells, and Dick Diver's return to America for his father's funeral combines leave-taking both of his father and of his homeland as he remembered it. Reverend Diver is buried in Virginia, along with generations of his family, a significant clue to Dick's past. The Divers have a history and, in a deep sense, they belong to the land. But either because Dick Diver knows that he has been severed from that tradition or that America herself has forsaken the memory of its first settlers. Dick bids a poignant farewell in Chapter xix: "Good-bye, my father—good-bye, all my fathers."

The ghosts of Dick's past seem to file before him on this voyage, as if, by their change, to indicate to Dick Diver his own change. On the voyage back to Europe he encounters Albert McKisco, the haughty and egocentric author who once fancied himself a kind of James Joyce when he and the Divers lived on the Riviera. McKisco, now, it seems, is all the rage. His novels are widely acclaimed, and with the lionizing of the literary world, McKisco seems to have become more interesting. But he is still a sham, and Dick Diver must wonder about a world that kills its Abe Norths but lets its Albert McKiscos survive.

Since Fitzgerald seems to be relentlessly knocking away at all of Dick Diver's props of hope and optimism, it is probably self-evident that on this trip the hero will have to reencounter Rosemary Hoyt, since, in some respects, it was his love for her which initially started the avalanche of unfortunate events which now threatens to bury Dick. She appears in the lobby of the Hotel Quirinal in Rome. Dick's first thoughts after seeing her are very telling; he desires to see her as she was in the past and "to hold her eloquent giving-of-herself in its precious shell, till he enclosed it, till it no longer existed outside him." In short, so precious in his memory of Rosemary's utter naïveté and selflessness when she first offered herself to him that in an attempt to preserve such simplicity, Dick would like to completely surround it, no doubt suffocating her in the process. Dick Diver, of all people, should know that human beings cannot be put into a hermetically sealed environment and be expected to flourish. It is testimony to his desperation to find something basic in himself that he wants to capture Rosemary's innocent self and imprison it for himself.

But he is to find that her innocence no longer remains. Like the deaths of Abe North and his father, there has been a death in Rosemary. She says straightforwardly to him in Chapter xx: "I was just a little girl when I met you, Dick. Now I'm a woman." She probably means the distinction in several ways. Her career as an actress is flourishing and she is therefore no longer the Hollywood ingénue whose first film was a hit. She has a romance with her leading man, an Italian named Nicotera, and later she confesses that this man would like to marry her, though, thus far, she has resisted. And, last, there is the question of her physical virginity. Dick Diver has a deep need to know that he would be her first lover, almost as though the defloration of her would buy *him* innocence, an odd paradox, but one that still has its adherents. Rosemary teases him when he asks her about her lovers; there have been six hundred and forty others, she says. Actually, there have not, but she feels that he deserves such an answer for having even asked the question. She has always been willing to surrender her virginity to Dick, but by the time the opportunity comes, physical virginity means little to Rosemary. She is disappointed to find that the Dick Diver she has admired during three years seems to be quite like other men in pressing on her his sexual needs, and Dick himself realizes at nearly the same time that it is Nicole he really loves and that his infatuation with Rosemary is "self-indulgence." The realization comes late— after his infatuation with Rosemary has caused Nicole's near-breakdown and his own professional demise. Self-knowledge comes too slowly. Yet he somehow still needs to believe in her innocence, if only so that he can destroy it, and in order to punish her and himself, he invents a succession of likely suitors, at which Rosemary laughs. His attitude toward lovers for Rosemary is odd, for it seems to imply some sort of ownership or promise, and it is probably difficult for readers to sympathize completely with Fitzgerald's comment that imagining Rosemary's lovers was a way of "torturing himself." Likewise, there is a contradiction in the fact of his understanding how much he loves Nicole in which he says, "thoughts about Nicole, that she should die, sink into mental darkness, love another man, made him physically sick." That he could equate death and mental disease with infidelity is a key to Dick Diver—and possibly to F. Scott Fitzgerald. There is a humorous contradiction, as well, in the fact that Dick Diver is thinking this thought, getting sick at his stomach at the idea of Nicole's infidelity, after he has seduced a woman whom he has loved, certainly with sexual overtones, for three years. Rosemary and Dick, finally, learn something about themselves and each other. After a tense conversation at the end of Chapter xxi, they part, Rosemary to go on with her career and Dick to return to Nicole. Dick Diver says good-bye again, this time adding sadly, "I don't seem to bring people happiness any more." Dick Diver has been unable to purchase a new beginning by seizing Rosemary's once virginal innocence.

There is one final degradation for Dick Diver in Rome: he is doomed to be rescued one last time by Baby Warren. Twice before, Dick's fate was determined by her — when she "bought" a doctor, then a clinic, for Nicole. Now when Dick meets her in Rome, she is anxious to get Nicole away from Franz and Dick's clinic and to settle her in England because, in her opinion, the English are the most "balanced" people in the world. Baby is an Anglophile; once before (in Gstaad) she appeared in the company of two Englishmen, and later in the novel we learned that she was engaged to an Englishman. One can ponder the reason for her national preferences, but it does seem to be related to the Warren money's having been made in one generation and having therefore no rank or class attached. It is almost as though Baby Warren would like to buy status through her love of the English.

Dick Diver has no innate love of the English, and, far from thinking them the sanest people in the world, he opposes Nicole's being moved to England because of a pious hope that the much vaunted English stability will aid her. He turns clinical psychologist by telling Baby frankly that Nicole's past has, in some ways, been inevitable. If the Diver marriage proves to be unsuccessful, she would have married someone like Dick anyway — someone, the undertone seems to be, of an independent cast whose lifeblood she could drain. Almost automatically Baby Warren's money-oriented self reacts: "You think she'd be happier with somebody else? Of course it could be arranged." Both Baby Warren and Dick Diver are wrong about Nicole, of course, and their coolly deciding her future, each in his own way, equates them for a moment. Nicole does not, in the end, set-tle for a father-figure or an Englishman, though it could be ques-tioned whether her ultimate choice is really better than the options which Baby and Dick have in mind for her.

The shallow and self-centered Baby Warren, whose main stability is the power she can buy with her wealth is, ironically, the only person Dick Diver can turn to when, later that evening, he gets thrown into jail because of hitting a man who, it turns out, is a plainclothes carabinieri, or Italian policeman. Far from possessing the old charm which characterized the early Dick Diver, the novel's hero rages, curses, and attacks because of what seems to be a simple matter of a cab fare. Unable to speak Italian, he is locked up like any other unruly citizen, and he must wait for Baby to come to help him.

Baby Warren is finally reached by Dick's emissary, and im-mediately she sets out to rescue him. She begins, typically enough for a woman who understands power and the ways of in-fluence, with the American Embassy. There she meets her match, a man of "the Eastern seaboard," not one of the Chicago *nouveau riche*, the class to which the Warrens belong. This employee is able to turn Baby away by his simple command that she leave; and the humor of the situation is amplified by the man's puny presence—he is swathed in pink cream, turbaned, and decked out in delicate nightclothes. Baby Warren does not give up, however, and later in the morning she is able to make the consul himself bow to her demands for American interces-sion to release Dick.

Fitzgerald injects a remarkable and altogether unexpected passage at this point, for it is prose of real hate. He equates Baby Warren with American womanhood; as he describes her trying to persuade the consul to come with her to free her brother-in-law he says: "The American Woman, aroused, stood over him; the clean-sweeping irrational temper that had broken the moral back of a race and made a nursery out of a continent, was too much for him." On the surface this seems an unworthy and gratuitous jibe, since to this point the reader has in no way been prepared for the judgment that Baby Warren is the symbol of American womanhood. She is not the only American woman in the book, so her attributes have not seemed to universalize her. We have not, until now, heard Fitzgerald's pronouncement that America is doomed, and we are not prepared for his judgment that the collapse has come because of women in America. As an outburst of authorial judgment this section deserves more to be included in a history of F. Scott Fitzgerald's ideas or a critical reading of his life than it does to contribute to the novel; it appears as an unwelcome incursion and is never followed up and, therefore, explains nothing.

Despite, or perhaps because of, her attacks on the virility of America, Baby Warren (with a vice-consul and a lawyer provided by the American Embassy) is nonetheless able to free Dick from his incarceration. The act has not, however, come without its penalty — Dick now knows that he is forever in her debt and that she will use this event in the future, if it is to her advantage. Baby Warren thinks that, at last, Dick is in her power; it is a measure of Dick's complete loss of self that he probably would not quarrel with that judgment. Far from discovering his essential self, Dick Diver, at the end of Book 2, is released from jail, but not from the prison of his own increasingly pathless life.

BOOK 3

This final segment of *Tender is the Night* strips away the two last, and most important, parts of Dick Diver's life — his wife and his profession. Fitzgerald seems to be creating a modern King Lear, who, bereft of his lands and possessions, loved ones, and even clothing, stands shivering on the heath. Like Lear's degradation, that of Dick Diver's is a process at once inexorable and moving.

It begins in Chapter i with a brief conversation between Kaethe and Franz Gregorovius which reveals much about these two characters and imparts to the reader the knowledge of what Dick must confront when he returns to Switzerland. Kaethe is unquestionably jealous of Nicole's beauty and wealth; Nicole, by the same token, is scornful of Kaethe and has no patience with her plodding domestic character. Kaethe is deeply aware of that scorn and tells her husband that Nicole treats her as if she smelled bad. In a way, the seeds of Dick's ultimate failure at the clinic are germinating in the relationship between the wives of the partners, suggesting that Dick himself will not be entirely to blame for what happens. The example of King Lear is not altogether without aptness, for, like Lear, Dick's demise comes both because of the flaws in his own character and because of external circumstances over which he has no control. Franz Gregorovius, it is clear, is an ambitious man, and he is waiting for an opportunity to manage the clinic by himself. Dick Diver returns, then, to an ambitious partner and his jealous wife.

After his debacle in Rome, however, Dick Diver seems more anxious than ever to achieve distinction in his career, and at his return he ambitiously throws himself into his work. Events overtake him, nonetheless; he seems fated to fail, particularly after the death of the Iron Maiden. Dick was very fond of her, we know, but more than that, it seems that in her death there died an idea, the belief that a woman could exist by and of herself. Again the ambivalence in F. Scott Fitzgerald's own attitude surfaces, for the death of a patient under ordinary circumstances should not be so completely upsetting to a doctor. It is possible that Dick—and Fitzgerald—wanted the Iron Maiden to survive in order to prove that a creative woman could live. She dies and, with her, dies an idea.

Ostensibly to give his partner a rest, Franz suggests that Dick make a trip to Lausanne to interview a prospective patient. What might have been a relaxing trip, however, turns into chaos. It has already been mentioned that in the Nicole/Dick/Iron Maiden scenes, Fitzgerald was examining the nature of the sexual bond between male and female. In this section of the book it becomes clear that Fitzgerald is occupied with the general topic of sexuality (though in no way can this, or any of Fitzgerald's works, be construed as "sexy" books). In Lausanne, Dick Diver encounters not one, but three instances of what he — and possibly Fitzgerald — views as unwholesome sexuality. The case which Dick is to examine involves a corrupt Spanish nobleman, Real (which, in Spanish, means "royal," not "reality"), whose son Francisco is a homosexual. The father wants his son to be "cured." Fitzgerald here is echoing a common attitude both of his time and ours — that is, homosexuality is illness or a perversion of "natural" heterosexual love. It need hardly be noted that the heterosexual relationships in this novel are, without exception, failures; if they are "natural," they are no happier than "unnatural" ones.

The father of Francisco, however, has been so adamant about making his son conform to his idea of normalcy that he has forced him to make a tour of bordellos. The inhumanity of such an act has two dimensions — that of forcing the young man, against his will, to perform sexually, and, equally as degrading, the assumption that the prostitution of females is somehow natural and healthy. When the boy was not cured by the experience, Senor Real was reduced to lashing him with a whip. The homosexuality seems, to Dick, an incurable sickness, and the father's cruelty a sexual perversion as well. Fitzgerald does not discuss the sickness of prostitution.

The perverse cruelty of the father/son relationship is a parallel to the perverse sexuality of Nicole's father with his young daughter; and, as if to force the parallel, Fitzgerald has Dick discover that Mr. Warren happens to be, at that very time, living in Lausanne and, it is presumed, dying. The revelation of the fact comes from Royal Dumphry, the effeminate young man on the Riviera in Book 1, who in this section is Francisco's lover.

Dick Diver, stunned by the news of Warren's illness, rushes to the bedside of his father-in-law, and as he sits talking to him, he hears a father's plea to see his daughter. But once again Dick must answer both as Nicole's husband and as her doctor; he says that, since his wife is not yet well, he will have to ask Franz's medical opinion.

Whether it is fate or mere bad judgment, Dick delivers the message by phone to Kaethe, forgetting until later to tell her to keep the fact from Nicole, though he trusts that she will have the good sense to be silent until Nicole can hear the news from Franz. Dick has misjudged Kaethe and Nicole's relationship, however, for Kaethe, knowing the information, goes up the mountain and, by chance, encounters Nicole. She draws her arm across Nicole's shoulder, and the woman recoils; the rebuff so angers Kaethe that she angrily reveals the truth to Nicole: her father is dying in nearby Lausanne. Nicole catches a train immediately, to find that her father has fled. Chapter ii ends with Nicole and Dick sitting in a bar listening to "The Wedding of the Painted Doll," significantly ironic under the circumstances, since it is symbolic of Nicole's arrested sexual development which, nonetheless, has not kept her from a marriage as brittle and as certain to collapse as a dollhouse marriage.

The phrase also echoes what is becoming a theme of infantility in the novel: Nicole, as a doll, and her sister, as "Baby," the American Woman as responsible for reducing the country to a "nursery," Rosemary Hoyt early in her career as "Daddy's Girl," and even Violet McKisco's being "charmed about the little discoveries that well-bred girls make in their teens." All these references point to Fitzgerald's preoccupation with the female's destructive immaturity, a malevolence made more insidious by its being under an exterior of infantile innocence. It is interesting to note that only women are cast into this role of infantility. Senor Real's son, while Fitzgerald obviously disapproves of him, is not accused by the author or by Dick Diver of arrested development; Dick dismisses Francisco only as a "little devil."

The end of Dick Diver's professional life is petty and anticlimactic, and for a person of Dick Diver's one-time promise, it could only be humiliating. Franz Gregorovius does not have to plot or plan at any length to get rid of his associate, for one of the patients' parents, Mr. Morris, accuses Dick of having alcohol on his breath and makes a scene on the hospital grounds, summarily driving off with his son without a doctor's permission.

Dick Diver suspects the truth about himself, that the high level of tension at the hospital has made him tipple too freely.

It is the remaining puritanical, reasonable, and firm side of Dick which makes him resolve not to drink any more, after he has realized, in the wake of the Morris episode, that his attackers have a point about his pretending to be able to cure alcoholics when he himself is uncertain about his own ability to tolerate it. But the decision is, of necessity, a shallow one because he decides only that his drinking is unprofessional and indiscreet, not that it is a basic problem.

But Franz Gregorovius is at least an opportunist and takes the occasion of Dick's confession of the scene with the Morrises to suggest that Dick go on another "leave of abstinence." His English is incorrect, but his meaning is thoroughly accurate. Dick realizes Franz's feelings and leaves the clinic, absenting himself finally from the serious practice of his profession.

Dick Diver's drinking becomes more intense. Even understanding how Fitzgerald was trapped in the problem of alcohol, one must admit that, for Dick Diver, alcoholism seems to be more a manifestation of deeper problems than a sickness in itself. That rationale was one which Fitzgerald himself used when, refusing to give up alcohol, he would insist that he was not addicted but, rather, was only using it to cope with his many problems, problems not, by the way, of his own making. Since the earlier and more secure Dick Diver had not needed to use alcohol, the assumption that Fitzgerald wants us to make is that his very need for it suggests that his life has gotten out of control; his drinking is supposed to be more a sign of a problem than a problem of itself.

Alcohol and wealth precipitate the conclusion of the Diver marriage, for the already significant fortune which Nicole brought to the marriage is increased by the sale of Dick's share of the clinic. Wealth, at this point in their marriage, as a contrast to an earlier period, translates itself into material possessions. In Chapter iv, Fitzgerald uses authorial intrusion ("Regard them, for example,") to describe how weighted down the Divers' life has become with the freight of their possessions. At a railway station their debarkation resembles a medieval pilgrimage, and, at their first stop in Italy, the complexity increases even more when they are met by the princely entourage of Abe North's widow, now the Contessa di Minghetti.

Mary North Minghetti's new name has cast away her identity as certainly as Abe North's fastened him to an American past, for Mary's new husband, the Count, is an Asiatic of the "Kyble-Berber-Sabaean-Hindu strain"; his origins span the continents of Asia and Africa, but his name is, contradictorily enough, a papal title conferred on him because of his wealth. There is a kind of poetic justice in the fact that Abe North's widow's new husband is dark enough so that he could not "travel in a pull-man south of the Mason-Dixon." The North and the South, symbolically, have met and married and, at the same time, magnanimously brought in the bloodlines of Europe, Asia, and Africa as well.

These bloodlines have created a household which the Divers, upon their arrival as a family, find inscrutable. The com-bination of boredom and alcohol cause Dick Diver to commit a *faux pas* of major proportions, an error that the younger, more socially integrated Dick would never have stumbled into. And, as before, Fitzgerald is writing about an incident from his own life. Scottie, while visiting Gerald and Sara Murphy with her parents, refused to bathe because she thought the water looked dirty and had probably been used to bathe the Murphy children before her. Actually, Sara Murphy said later that the addition of bath crystals made the water look cloudy, and that she would never have thought of bathing two people successively in the same water. The same episode, woven into the story of the Divers' stay at the Minghettis' has the added drama of Dick's accusing a "maid" of not giving his son Lanier clean bath water. Because Dick had been drunk when introductions were being made, he did not realize that the "maid" was the Count's sister, and the humiliation resulting from such an insult was profound to the woman. Rather than apologizing for his errors, or at least using humor or his former self-assured and graceful cajolery, he asks his son to reassert the dirty bathwater story. When Mary says, "If you'd only listened . . ." Dick carelessly replies, "But

you've gotten so damn dull, Mary," thus alienating an old acquaintance, as well as her new husband. The entire Diver family
must leave immediately, in disgrace.

There is no sane and protected place for the Divers from
this point onward. Back at their Riviera home, the French cook
Augustine, in Chapter v, goes on a rampage, drinking and threat-
ening to kill Dick with a chef's knife when he attempts to dismiss her. That even a servant can threaten Dick Diver's life
shows the extent of his degradation. After the cook is duly fired,
Nicole, later at a dinner in Nice, observes, "you used to want
to create things—now you seem to want to smash them up."
The accusation seems true.

Several corrupt and vapid characters enter the last chapters
of the book as if to make Dick's demise even more empty. On a
whim, having boarded a yacht belonging to a man named Golding, Dick and Nicole meet Tommy Barban again and are introduced for the first time to Lady Caroline Sibley-Biers. Fitzgerald
seems to introduce the latter as if to undermine Baby Warren's
judgment that the English people are the most balanced people
in the world. Lady Caroline is decadent, vapid, and downright
evil, as the words in the silly jazz song she has written suggest:
"there was a young lady from hell." The shipboard party is a
scene which is difficult to fathom; the reader's principal feeling
at the end of the description of the singing, drinking, and merriment is that there is an indescribable desperation, and Dick,
rather than absenting himself or, on the other hand, comporting
himself with humor and grace, ends up insulting people, drinking too much, and refusing to tone down his comments. At one
point, Nicole misses him, and perhaps fearful that he has tossed
himself overboard, goes to find him; at seeing him, standing
quite still at the front of the boat, she bursts into tears, tears of
relief and of genuine sorrow for the man who has changed so.

In Chapter vi, Fitzgerald attempts to change the tempo of
the story too quickly: he must show Dick so defeated and Nicole
so strong that her decision to leave with Tommy Barban will be
believable. This section is one that we are insufficiently prepared

for; during the scene on the yacht, Nicole is sane and in control
of herself, quite inexplicably, and the reader has never been
told how this manifest strength and sanity came about. If Fitzgerald wants us to believe that Nicole is healthy because Dick
is unhealthy, the situation which would support the principle
of transference, but there has never been any dramatic proof;
at no point has the reader seen that at the same time Dick dis-
integrated, Nicole was being reborn.

After the riotous scene on the yacht, the action returns to
the Villa Diana, where Tommy has driven the Divers after the
party. Dick awakens apologetic about the night before, and
Tommy, who has spent the night with them, is worried about the
effects of the gathering on Nicole. Dick, certain of his wife's
health, says, "Nicole is now made of— of Georgia pine, which is
the hardest wood known, except lignum vitae from New Zea-
land—." With this analogy, we feel that Nicole is healed. Yet
what Fitzgerald emphasizes is that Nicole has gotten hard, not
healthy. And the fact remains that it is not easy to understand
her change in either case.

Just as Nicole's sudden sanity is insufficiently prepared for,
so is her amorous preference for Tommy Barban something of
a surprise. From the first pages of the novel, the reader has
known that Tommy is in love with Nicole, but never has the
reciprocal case been true. The decisive action which marks her
love is a trivial one. At this departure she gives him a full jar
of camphor rub to use for his sore throat, despite Dick's pro-
testations that the stuff is difficult to obtain because it has to
be imported.

Presumably the camphor rub scene informs the reader that
Nicole has a natural impulse for Tommy. The only thing that
is really clear, however, is that Nicole is increasingly embar-
rassed for Dick. Chapter vii shows Dick Diver's attempts at
feats of strength as an acute reversal of his physical and mental
acumen of Book 1. Rosemary Hoyt has once more appeared on
the scene, and, rather like a testy adolescent, Dick tries repeatedly to show off for her. While riding a board behind a boat,

he tries to stand up and lift a man on his shoulders. He fails repeatedly, but, not giving up, keeps trying. Finally when he is hauled aboard, the women feel they must make excuses for him. Dick has also given up high diving, a significant fact, given his name, and the former wit and humor in his conversations have been replaced by self-jibes and carelessness of others' feelings.

Dick Diver's decision to go to Provence for a few days creates an opportunity for Nicole and Tommy to initiate their affair; Chapter viii opens with Nicole's preparations for him. Having "anointed" herself, she looks in the mirror and finds herself still beautiful, though no longer young. Fitzgerald points out that she is jealous of young girls because the movies show the "myriad faces of the girl-children, blandly represented as carrying on the word and wisdom of the world." This is yet another clue to the destructiveness of a woman masquerading as a child and thereby causing everyone harm.

The actual seduction scene itself has less to say about the act than about the change in the two characters performing it. Tommy immediately tells Nicole that she has "white crook's eyes." She is offended at first, then, considering, says that if that is the case, it is because she is well again and looking like her heritage, for her grandfather was a crook, and she might likely resemble one. Nicole's character has now proceeded from normalcy and sanity to that of viciousness and evil. Tommy is able to have his will with her, and they are off to Nice. During the trip, Nicole thinks, significantly, "So I have white crook's eyes, have I? Very well, then, better a sane crook than a mad puritan," a phrase obviously intended to dismiss Dick and all he has stood for in her life. Excited by the idea of the affair, Nicole urges Tommy to stop before they get to Nice, and there the seduction takes place. Afterward, Tommy looks at her body and compares it to that of a new baby, by now a metaphor of Fitzgerald's for all womanhood. The scene's infantile immorality is enhanced by a scene of girls, screeching to their lovers who are departing from the harbor. The quality of Tommy and Nicole's love is equally as thoughtless.

Nicole, upon Dick's return, seems to give him one last chance to replace Tommy's new position in her life. In Chapter ix, she goes to Dick's study cottage, remembering Tommy's embraces and, Fitzgerald says, "with the opportunistic memory of women," forgetting that she had had such joy with Dick once upon a time before they were married. She intends to approach him to renew their acquaintance. He rebuffs her with "Don't touch me!" Then he adds, "I can't do anything for you any more. I'm trying to save myself." The battle they have, then, is entirely that of souls; it is fought quietly, and Nicole wins. How she wins seems uncertain, since it is clear that she will, as a result of her victory, simply place herself in bondage to a new man. Nonetheless, the effect on Dick is considerable. He no longer has his patient. Of course, for the departure of Nicole to be as heartrending as it must, one must substitute "loved wife" for "patient."

Dick Diver has one last chance to be his former self, and he does so, but this time with a difference. He is called out of bed by an agent of the police because Mary North Minghetti and Lady Caroline Sibley-Biers have been arrested for impersonating men and, under that guise, picking up women. Mary is dreadfully frightened lest her husband learn of the escapade; Lady Caroline is arrogant and insulting. Dick manages to solve the situation by lying to the police and by bribing them with money borrowed from the owner of Gausse's Hotel. Mary, once freed, promises to repay her share as soon as possible, but Lady Caroline refuses, and, in an action designed to please everyone, Mr. Gausse walks up behind Lady Caroline and "swiftly planted his foot in the most celebrated of targets." In a way, however, the scene is like that after the Divers' auto accident: the actual physical violence against the woman seems almost to be something Fitzgerald himself would have liked to have done.

The separation of husband and wife comes at the barber's. Tommy comes to deliver his threat: Nicole must come with him because she no longer loves her husband. Dick, half-shaven, must leave the barber chair to hear this claim, and he yields without giving Tommy the row he expects — and desires.

In Chapter xii, Dick bids farewell to the Riviera. The scene is touchingly written, with Dick embracing the gardener and spending the day with his children so that he will remember them, then walking about the terrace talking in a desultory way, though he knows that Nicole and Baby are there with Tommy. Nicole makes one last effort to go to him, but Tommy orders her back.

Chapter xiii should read as the postmortem of a man who still walks the earth. Shakespeare was wont to strew the final scene of his tragedies with bodies, dead and dying; Fitzgerald need not speak of the living death of Dick Diver in any but the most casual terms. His hero has been reduced to living from one small town to the next, from petty scandal to hopeless job, and, saddest of all, he must always survive with the knowledge that he once had promise, like Grant in Galena.

Character Analyses

DICK DIVER

Mankind seems always to have been concerned with the problem of failure, for Western literature abounds with stories of a fall from a state of goodness and promise. In its Hellenic roots, failure was discussed in the great tragedies; in its Judaeo-Christian roots, failure began with man's fall from God's grace. There is no need to discuss whether, in Dick Diver, Fitzgerald was intending to create a prototype of the historical tragic hero. It is enough to know that the author was working within a long tradition in order to create this tale of failure in the twentieth century.

Classically, characters fall for one of two reasons or, most frequently, from a combination of the two — because of fate, which rules that what will be will be, and because of a character flaw, or human frailty, which causes people to err, thus leading to their doom. Dick Diver, like a Shakespearean hero, is a victim both of external circumstances and the flaws in his own character.

There is an additional likeness to classic tradition in Dick Diver's original state before his fall from fame. It has often been argued that the most moving tragedy involves a fall from a high place, from a position of esteem and promise. At the beginning of his career, Dick seems dauntless, a veritable golden boy: his education has been excellent and his future as a psychiatrist is a respected one in the dawning years of that profession. His residency in Switzerland places him in Europe, where the great Freud and Jung were located. In the days after the close of the war, Dick Diver's future seemed full of hope — like that of Grant's in Galena.

His marriage to Nicole, however, introduces the complicating external circumstances. Nicole brings wealth, which becomes a serious deterrent to Dick's career, since it determines his social class, the kind of patients he will deal with, the sorts of friends he will have, and the social circles in which he will move. Even his location is determined by Nicole's wealth, since the clinic has been, in a sense, purchased for Dick. He has to live with the crippling realization that it has been Warren money, not his own professional reputation, which has provided him a place to practice psychiatry.

Nicole's money leads to Dick's being used by her family, as well. He is in a human situation, a marriage, where he must always be on duty. The character of Nicole is not sufficiently developed, but it is clear that her very presence drains Dick's strength. By transference—that is, directing her childhood feelings to a new object, in this case her husband—Nicole requires that Dick simultaneously be her father, guide, and physician, as well as her spouse. The demand would be too great for anyone, and the many roles he must play exhaust Dick.

That Dick Diver ever submitted to the marriage in the first place suggests one of the flaws in his character. He chose to marry a woman whose history he knew and the course of whose mental illness he could have predicted. His capacity to love Nicole, far from a weakness, should be considered a credit to his humanity. What is a limitation is his inability to judge matters in the light of his own self-interest. Indeed, one of Dick's friends at the university warned "that's going to be your trouble —judgment about yourself." Just as he finally realized that his infatuation with Rosemary Hoyt was "self-indulgence," so might he have realized that marriage to Nicole would be an encumbrance to his future. He could have chosen not to marry a mental patient who was also an heiress.

His succumbing to Nicole suggests that Dick Diver had, on the one hand, a weakness for beauty and, on the other, a deep need for approval and love. To love and be loved constitutes a healthy human relationship, but Dick seems to want love so much that he will destroy himself to get it. His very social charm springs from a kind of self-effacing desire to put others at their ease so that they will like themselves and him as well.

Critics have frequently charged that it is Dick Diver's weakness for wealth that leads to his downfall. What seems to be more important, however, is that Nicole's money dictates his lifestyle. Dick does not have the strength to ignore the leisure that money can buy, and his commitment to his work erodes thereby and, with it, the requisite self-esteem.

Indeed, it is possible that Dick Diver's most serious flaw is a lack of discipline in regard to his work. After his life seems to have been loosed from its moorings, Dick turns often to his work, but his career never progresses, possibly because he has no lasting commitment to it. His first book, it should be noted, was a handbook that has become a standard text in the field. His *oeuvre* was not a creative effort but rather an integrative compendium of information. Likewise, his second projected work has a verbose and inflated-sounding title which will, Fitzgerald points out in a footnote, look especially impressive in German. Dick has a bit of Albert McKisco in him, for his two books, while not altogether derivatory, have not emerged from a period of absorbing research to become pioneering, thought-provoking efforts. After his marriage to Nicole, Dick seems unable to settle down to work in anything more than a kind of dilatory way. And the presence of Nicole is not really an excuse for relaxing his professional efforts, since after the divorce, instead of starting over in earnest, he even leaves his original calling.

Dick Diver's most serious lapse, then, is a spiritual one. He could have done great work in his field if he had been disciplined in the practice of his profession and in his application to his writing. Had he been that disciplined, a saving measure of self-awareness might have kept him from Nicole Warren, whose wealth and illness diverted his life from its true intellectual track, that "fine quiet of the scholar which is nearest of all things to heavenly peace."

NICOLE DIVER

Like Daisy Buchanan in *The Great Gatsby*, Nicole Diver seems less a fully developed character than a vehicle to help account for the downfall of a man. One often has the feeling that F. Scott Fitzgerald's female characters are a projection of one or another side of Zelda, but that in no one of them was he able to successfully portray his wife completely and with veracity.

Nicole Diver's portrayal begins with her childhood history, when she was violated by her father after her mother's death. She remains a child in the Diver marriage largely because she transfers her feelings of paternal authority to Dick Diver. When she seems to outgrow Dick at the end of the novel, she is actually only placing herself in bondage to another, less worthy, man. She lives out the song which she plays to Dick on the hospital grounds before their marriage, for the lyrics conclude: "Just like a silver dollar goes from hand to hand, / A woman goes from man to man."

As has been pointed out in the foregoing critical commentary, Nicole Diver's illness is drawn from Zelda Fitzgerald's own case history, a fact which weakens her in many ways because Fitzgerald seems unable to distance himself sufficiently from his own wife to draw a credible fictional creation. Nicole is revealed first by her letters to Dick, letters which initially exhibit serious instability, then gradually lead to her confession that she would like someone to love her, a sign that she has improved, since a hatred of men might be expected of a victim of incest.

She still seems a child as she waits perfumed and nervous for Dick on the hospital grounds. In the sections after their marriage, her coherency flashes on and off so much that is is difficult to detect much growth in her as a character.

Fitzgerald is unconvincing when he tries to show that Nicole is the agent of Dick Diver's tragedy because Fitzgerald never allows her real maturity; when she does change, she does so too rapidly. Although she shows her husband tenderness on the Golding yacht and she is understanding about his need to impress Rosemary in the last chapters, she is almost immediately thrust into a role of evil. Fitzgerald's description of her eyes being "white crook's eyes" is thrust upon us, making her no longer childish but wicked. Fitzgerald seems to allow her evil eyes to be discovered by Tommy Barban to indicate that Dick has always been able to bring out some good in her, while, with Tommy, she releases her unrestrained self.

During her brief affair with Tommy, Nicole changes; she has known that Dick has been viewing her with growing indifference and that a crisis is due. The affair releases her sexual energy, and she approaches Dick for a major confrontation. At this point in the novel, Fitzgerald describes Nicole as being filled with arrogance because of her wealth and a detestation of Dick's past attempts to minister to her; she has used Dick the physician, flaunting her wealth and beauty before him. What makes her character even more confusing is that after she has finally triumphed over Dick, she tries in the last Riviera scene to go back to him but is restrained by Tommy. Either she has not rejected Dick as completely as she thought she had or, what is more likely, she is an inveterate victim, a pawn of men who hand her, like a shining silver dollar, from one hand to the next.

ROSEMARY HOYT

Rosemary Hoyt is continually associated with the movies not only because she is an actress and is actually seen on the set, but also because her vision is oddly cinematic. In the 1951 version of the novel, the chapter told from her point of view is called "Rosemary's Angle." Just as the word "angle" describes the range or tilt of a camera lens, so are her perceptions broad-ranging and photographically superficial at first glance. When she scans the people on the Riviera beach she sees the drama immediately, and when she falls in love with Dick, she does so precipitously, almost as if she were performing in a two-hour matinee. But just as a photograph can suggest rich and imaginative dramatic possibilities, so are Rosemary's often seemingly superficial responses often more profound than she knows. Fitzgerald uses these early innocent perceptions of Rosemary's to sharpen the descriptions of the other characters.

Rosemary develops only minimally within the novel, moving from an immature, childish starlet uncertain of her future to a fairly self-assured star, certain of her future. She will, however, remain content to live in a man's world. She seems, in the last scenes, prepared to marry her leading man and live happily ever after in the best Hollywood tradition.

Themes and Symbols

THE SEXUAL METAPHOR

While incest has often been cited as a theme of *Tender is the Night,* it has less frequently been seen as part of a larger pattern of sexual relationships in the novel. Incest as a theme is pervasive; it recurs again and again, from Devereux and Nicole Warren in its blatant physicality to its artistic manifestation in Rosemary's movie, *Daddy's Girl,* to its psychological level in Dick Diver's relationship both to Nicole and Rosemary, each of whom plays a girl-child to his father role.

But incest, psychological or physical, is part of a larger pattern of sexual roles in this novel. One is reminded of Sylvia Plath's "Daddy" in the *Ariel* poems, where "daddy" comes to stand for her own father, her husband, and Hitler, and finally for power, control, and even oppression. Fitzgerald says early in the novel that in Paris, Dick Diver was surrounded by women —Rosemary, Nicole, Violet McKisco, and Mary North—who "were all happy to exist in a man's world," therein differing from most American women. To exist in a man's world means, in each of these cases, that the woman allows herself to be managed by her mate or lover. When Abe North says that he is "tired of women's worlds," then, he probably means that he is tired of the passivity and lack of imagination exhibited by women.

Only two women in the novel stand outside this "women's world"—Baby Warren and the Iron Maiden. Dick, as we have seen, sympathizes deeply with the Iron Maiden and is deeply affected by her death. She perishes, Dick knows, because she tried to live in a man's world and failed. She does not have the endurance to be independent and creative. Baby Warren is the other character who does not live in a "woman's world" because she refuses to submit to any man; indeed, with the aid of her fortune, she labors to attain power over men. Significantly, she never marries.

The underlying dichotomy, then, is "woman's world" and "man's world," with the former standing for coherence and passivity, and the latter embodying creativity and dominance. Abe North needs a man's world in order to create; the Iron Maiden, because she is a woman, cannot exist in the raw world of the independent artist. One variation on this theme is provided by the homosexuals, who are male but reject the dominance and creativity due them and are generally treated scornfully for that reason. Another variation is offered by the American Woman, who, in one brief passage comes to be identified with Baby Warren; this creature unjustly usurps the dominant male role and, clumsily wielding her new-found power without its natural concomitant creativity, brings only destruction.

WAR

There are many references to war in the novel, references which provide a continuing metaphor for the disintegration of the Western world, as well as those which enrich the author's descriptions of Dick's state of mind. Dick Diver is associated with all three major American wars. He claims to be a descendant of Mad Anthony Wayne, a Revolutionary War hero. He is also compared, unfavorably it turns out, with Ulysses S. Grant, a Civil War hero. And Dick himself notes after a bad dream that he suffers from "non-combatant's shell-shock" after World War I.

As has been stated in the foregoing critical commentary, the first World War is described by Dick as a "love war" because it represented for both sides the eager defense of a way of life, a culture that had been centuries in the making. In the aftermath of the war, the Western world lay in disarray. Dick Diver has internalized that sorrow and fragmentation, and, as a result, he comes to typify a man of the Western world who is left to survive after its most devastating war.

MOON

In the revisions which Fitzgerald sketched out for his reorganization of the novel, there is the cryptic phrase—"change moon" after the first chapter revision. Malcolm Cowley confessed to never finding this exact reference, but the notation suggests that Fitzgerald probably saw the moon as an important symbolic vehicle in the narrative.

Some of Fitzgerald's most poetic and flowing language is associated with descriptions of darkness, moonlight, and sunlight in the novel, and a complex interplay between them begins to emerge. The sunshine often glares down on the beach, revealing the dramatic action of the novel. The dark night, often illuminated by the moon, seems by the same token to suggest the erotic and mysterious underside of human action.

While the moon becomes progressively associated with passionate love, in one case it suggests a kind of artistic desperation. This occurrence is the song performed by Lanier and Topsy in Chapter vi of Book 1; it is the popular "Mon Ami Pierrot," the verse of which they sing roughly translates as:

My friend Pierrot, fetch me your pen to
Write a word by the light of the moon.
My candle is out; I have no more
Light. Open the door for the love of God.

The song seems to suggest that in darkness caused by the extinguished candle, the artist sets down his word only by the light of the moon. The moon is evanescent, shining only occasionally on a world otherwise either dark or blindingly lit by the sun.

THE TITLE

F. Scott Fitzgerald was always deeply moved by John Keats's poetry, and even in the course of this novel he shows

Dick Diver's "spirit soar" as he pauses at the house in Rome where Keats died. The lines from Keats's "Ode to a Nightingale" which give the novel its title are inscribed on the title page, but exactly why Fitzgerald chose that particular poem or those particular lines is something of a mystery.

There are references within the novel to a nightingale, suggesting that the same influences which Keats describes as transforming him as he sat listening to the bird's song are also working upon the characters in the novel. When Abe North is trying to describe why McKisco agreed to duel with Tommy Barban, he says that McKisco was "probably plagued by the nightingale," meaning that, as in Keats's case, the nightingale's song encourages thoughts of death and immortality. Later, the cricket's song has much the same effect on Nicole and Dick as it holds "the scene together with a single note." A last, perhaps confusing fact is that in her novel, *Save Me the Waltz*, Zelda Fitzgerald calls the Riviera home that Fitzgerald names the Villa Diana, "Les Rossignols," which in French means "the nightingales." To both Fitzgeralds, then, the nightingale seems to have been an emblem of their Riviera experience.

It is significant that Fitzgerald deletes two lines from the section of the ode which he quotes. They are: "And haply the Queen-Moon is on her throne,/ Cluster'd around by all her starry Fays." In Keats's poem these lines suggest a kind of saving optimism, the thought that perhaps somewhere the moon and stars are shining brilliantly, although the poet himself is cloaked in darkness, unable even to see the flowers at his feet. The "tender night" of the poet is without a moon, and the song of the bird has brought him to this trancelike state of suspended time, when his thoughts are on death and immortality.

The moon, in Fitzgerald's *Tender is the Night*, is often an elusive symbol, whether or not it can be identified with Keats's Queen Moon. It comes to punctuate time often in the person of a young and beautiful woman or, not surprisingly, during scenes of love. Rosemary awakens during the night she first falls in love with Dick Diver, and the time is described as a "limpid black night," just as it is in Keats's evocation, though Rosemary, awaking, is "suspended in the moonshine." In this instance, Rosemary seems almost to become identified with the Queen Moon of Keats's poem.

The other moon references in the novel occur largely with Nicole. In one of her letters to Dick before their marriage she says "I've thought a lot about moonlight too," suggesting some conspiracy of knowledge between them about the effect of the moon on human beings. Later, as Dick falls more in love with her, they meet on the sanitarium grounds, and as the young and beautiful Nicole comes to meet Dick, she comes out of the woods into "clear moonlight," a kind of goddess of youth and beauty. Although the moon is not specifically mentioned, sexual love between Nicole and Dick is suggested by such a phrase as "between the loves of the white nights," a transforming act after which Nicole feels bereft and alone. And after she has left Dick for the affair with Tommy, their sexual unions are described as "tangled with love in the moonlight."

The phrase "tender is the night" suggests the dominant mood of the novel, in that the characters are often shrouded in darkness, literal and metaphorical. Their motives, their actions, and their very lives are not illuminated by optimism or self-knowledge. When the moon sheds its light, a romance ensues even a period of illumination, but the romance passes too, leaving the bare world with its problems, a world in Keats's words:
    Where youth grows pale, and spectre-thin, and dies;
Where but to think is to be full of sorrow
    And leaden-eyed despairs,
Where Beauty cannot keep her lustrous eyes,
    Or new Love pine at them beyond tomorrow.

Discussion Questions and Essay Topics

1. Discuss the use of music in the novel, noting how a particular lyric or title of a popular song is used to suggest information.

2. List the dates mentioned in the novel, including the chronological age of the main characters. Is there any particular significance in the ages or the time period of the novel?

3. Discuss the McKisco-Barban duel and its significance on society and the characters involved.

4. Discuss why most of the action occurs in Europe. How does America function in the novel?

5. Discuss the recurring images of war in the novel.

6. Are the names of the characters significant? It is not wise to push this inquiry too far, but notice especially Diver, Barban, Abe North, Mary North Minghetti, Baby Warren, and the Iron Maiden.

7. How does Fitzgerald view homosexuality in the novel?

8. Dick Diver early in his career realizes that "the price of his intactness was incompleteness." Discuss his life in light of this phrase.

9. What does Fitzgerald mean by twice mentioning Grant in Galena in regard to Dick Diver?

10. Discuss the use of Rosemary Hoyt's perceptions to the progress of the novel.

11. Discuss the symbolic levels of the murder of Jules Peterson, the black shoeshine manufacturer from Scandinavia.

12. How does the character of the Iron Maiden function? What does her name mean? What does her malady symbolize?

13. Discuss Fitzgerald's use of English people in the novel, with special reference to Lady Caroline Sibley-Biers.

14. Discuss Nicole's heritage (the Warren family), as contrasted with that of the Diver family.

15. In what ways does Nicole Diver change in the novel?

16. Fitzgerald intended this to be his "psychological" novel. In what ways did he succeed in making it so, and in what ways did he fail?

17. Discuss the character of Baby Warren and the author's attitude toward her.

18. Discuss the use of movies, actresses, and actors in the novel.

19. What seems to be the function of Collis Clay as a character? Albert McKisco? Senor Real?

20. Why does Dick Diver fall in love with Rosemary? What are the consequences of his feelings?

21. How do Nicole and Dick Diver each respectively seem to relate to their children?

22. What kind of a woman is Elsie Speers?

23. Discuss the theme of incest in the novel, both its physical occurrrence and its symbolic dimensions.

24. Discuss Dick Diver's quest for innocence — why he needs it and what he finds.

25. Is Dick Diver, finally, a good man destroyed because of forces beyond his own control or because of the weaknesses in his own personality?

Selective Bibliography

There is a great deal of information for the student interested in Fitzgerald. Although the following list contains only full-length books, the examination of periodical articles are especially useful as well. There was a *Fitzgerald Newsletter* issued between 1958 and 1968 in forty numbers; it became the *Fitzgerald/Hemingway Annual* and contains interesting and valuable material. A bibliography of articles appears in *Modern Fiction Studies*, VII (Spring, 1961), and the annual bibliography of American literature in *Publications of the Modern Language Association* gives a yearly listing of articles on Fitzgerald.

For students interested in examining more of Fitzgerald's writings, two items deserve notice. Matthew Bruccoli's *F. Scott Fitzgerald: A Descriptive Bibliography* (Pittsburgh: University of Pittsburgh Press, 1972) is a lengthy, though still incomplete, listing of editions and writings. A broad collection of Fitzgerald's short writings from 1912 onward, showing the diversity of his talent, is found in Matthew J. Bruccoli and Jackson R. Bryer, eds., *F. Scott Fitzgerald in His Own Time* (Kent, Ohio: Kent State University Press, 1971). An excerpt appears in that volume from *Liberty* magazine in 1930 called "Girls Believe in Girls," which appears to have special relevance to *Tender is the Night*.

BIOGRAPHICAL MATERIAL

EBLE, KENNETH E. *F. Scott Fitzgerald.* New York: Twayne Publishing Co., 1963.

MIZENER, ARTHUR. *The Far Side of Paradise.* Boston: Houghton, Mifflin, 1951. The first thorough biography of Fitzgerald, and probably the best.

MIZENER, ARTHUR. *Scott Fitzgerald and His World*. New York: G. P. Putnam's Sons, 1972. If a picture is worth a thousand words, this collection of photographs, with its text, is educative as well as pleasurable.

MILFORD, NANCY. *Zelda: A Biography*. New York: Harper and Row, 1970. The popular, though well written and researched, biography of Zelda Sayre Fitzgerald.

PIPER, HENRY DAN. *Scott Fitzgerald: A Candid Portrait*. New York: Holt, Rinehart, and Winston, 1963.

TURNBULL, ANDREW. *Scott Fitzgerald: A Biography*. New York: Charles Scribner's Sons, 1962.

CRITICISM

BRUCCOLI, MATTHEW J. *The Composition of Tender is the Night*. Pittsburgh: University of Pittsburgh Press, 1963. Outlines the evolution of the various versions of the novel.

CALLAHAN, JOHN F. *The Illusions of a Nation: Myth and History in the Novels of F. Scott Fitzgerald*. Urbana: University of Illinois Press, 1972. An especially penetrating examination of the symbolic dimensions of Dick Diver.

KAZIN, ALFRED, ed. *F. Scott Fitzgerald: The Man and His Work*. Cleveland and New York: World, 1951. A collection of early Fitzgerald criticism.

LAHOOD, MARVIN J., ed. *Tender is the Night: Essays in Criticism*. Bloomington: Indiana University Press, 1969. An indispensable collection of relevant essays covering numerous aspects of the novel.

MILLER, JAMES E. *F. Scott Fitzgerald, His Art and Technique*. New York: New York University Press, 1964.

MIZENER, ARTHUR, ed. *F. Scott Fitzgerald: A Collection of Critical Essays.* Englewood Cliffs, N. J.: Prentice-Hall, 1963. Essays on a broad range of topics in regard to Fitzgerald's work.

STERN, MILTON R. *The Golden Moment: The Novels of F. Scott Fitzgerald.* Urbana: University of Illinois Press, 1970. Contains a very lengthy treatment of *Tender is the Night.*

NOTES

NOTES

NOTES